At Issue

Weapons of War

Other Books in the At Issue Series:

At Issue

Weapons of War

Diane Andrews Henningfeld, Book Editor

GREENHAVEN PRESS
A part of Gale, Cengage Learning

GALE
CENGAGE Learning

Detroit • New York • San Francisco • New Haven, Conn • Waterville, Maine • London

GALE
CENGAGE Learning

Elizabeth Des Chenes, *Managing Editor*

© 2012 Greenhaven Press, a part of Gale, Cengage Learning.

Gale and Greenhaven Press are registered trademarks used herein under license.

For more information, contact:
Greenhaven Press
27500 Drake Rd.
Farmington Hills, MI 48331-3535
Or you can visit our Internet site at gale.cengage.com

Articles in Greenhaven Press anthologies are often edited for length to meet page require-ments. In addition, original titles of these works are changed to clearly present the main thesis and to explicitly indicate the author's opinion. Every effort is made to ensure that Greenhaven Press accurately reflects the original intent of the authors. Every effort has been made to trace the owners of copyrighted material.

Cover image copyright © Images.com/Corbis.

LIBRARY OF CONGRESS CATALOGING-IN-PUBLICATION DATA

Weapons of War / Diane Andrews Henningfeld, book editor.
   p. cm. -- (At issue)
   Includes bibliographical references and index.
   ISBN 978-0-7377-5604-3 (hardcover) -- ISBN 978-0-7377-5605-0 (pbk.)
   1. Military weapons. 2. Weapons systems. 3. Military art and science. I. Henning-feld, Diane Andrews.
   UF500.W486 2011
   355.8--dc22
                                                                     2011010265

Printed in the United States of America
   1 2 3 4 5   15 14 13 12 11

FD224

Contents

Introduction

Intercontinental ballistic missiles (ICBMs) are perhaps the most fearsome and deadly of all weapons of war. Tipped with nuclear warheads, ICBMs promised mutual mass destruction to the superpowers of the Cold War during the years after World War II. Although they were never used, they provided a potent deterrent against all-out war throughout the latter half of the twentieth century. A typical ICBM could travel at well over 7,000 miles at high speed to deliver one or more nuclear blasts to an enemy target, causing massive destruction at the point of impact. The missiles were housed in silos across the United States or on nuclear submarines, and they remain an uncomfortable reminder that people have developed weapons that could wipe out all life on earth. In recognition of the danger posed by nuclear weapons, in 1991, the United States and Russia began disarming and destroying their arsenals of nuclear-equipped ICBMs, according to the terms of the first Strategic Arms Reduction Treaty.

In the first decades of the twenty-first century, however, new technologies have shifted the potential uses of missiles. Armed with non-nuclear warheads, the first-strike ICBM concept has morphed into a new program for weapons delivery called the "conventional prompt global strike system," or CPGS. CPGS weapons could potentially seek out and destroy any target on earth in under an hour. Coupled with a non-nuclear-missile-based defense system, the new missiles could lead to a steady and permanent reduction of nuclear weapon stockpiles, making the world safer at the same time.

According to "Investments in Conventional Prompt Global Strike," a December 2010 fact sheet from the US Department of State, the United States is developing "the capability to precisely strike time-sensitive, high-value targets" through the use of CPGS. David Sanger and Thom Shanker, writing in the

April 22, 2010, issue of *The New York Times*, suggest that such weapons might be called on for "tasks like picking off Osama bin Laden in a cave, if the right one could be found; taking out a North Korean missile while it is being rolled to the launch pad; or destroying an Iranian nuclear site."

The Pentagon is considering the development of several versions of the CPGS concept. Tony Allen-Mills, writing in the April 25, 2010, London *Sunday Times*, describes a possible scenario: "The new weapon could be launched from air, land or sea on a long-range missile travelling at suborbital altitudes about 350,000 ft. The missile releases a hypersonic pilotless plane that receives updates from satellites as it homes in on its target at up to five times the speed of sound." As Allen-Mills and other writers note, the weapon would inflict a devastating blow on its target; however, the precision of the weapon would mean that it would not cause the wide-scale, long-term mass destruction of a nuclear blast.

President Barack Obama supports the development of such weapons. In the Strategic Arms Reduction Treaty negotiations (START III) with Russia that took place in Prague in the spring of 2010, Obama agreed to a reduction of one US nuclear missile for every CPGS weapon added to the US arsenal, according to Allen-Mills. Thus, the new use of missiles would be within the terms of START III, ratified by the US Congress in early 2011. As stated by the US Department of State, "The New START Treaty allows the United States to deploy CPGS systems, and does not in any way limit or constrain research, development, testing and evaluation of such concepts and systems."

Not everyone is happy with the shift in US policy, however. There is concern that nations scanning for missile launches from the US might not be able to distinguish a CPGS launch from a full-scale nuclear launch. Such an error might lead to an unthinkably destructive war. The director of the Russian Nuclear Forces Project, Pavel Podvig, argues, "The short flight time [of the CPGS] ... leaves very little time for an assessment of the situation, putting an enormous strain on national decision-making mechanisms and increasing the probability of an accident" (quoted by Allen-Mills).

The United States has attempted to assure other nations of the world that safeguards will be put in place to prevent this kind of misunderstanding. "To remove some of the uncertainty from Conventional Prompt Global Strike (CPGS)," reports Paul Koring of *The Globe and Mail*, "one option under consideration is to locate all conventionally armed ballistic missiles at the Vandenberg Air Force base in California. That way, major powers like Russia and China that have the capacity to detect launches would know that a ballistic missile fired from there wasn't nuclear tipped."

Congressional Research Service nuclear weapons policy specialist Amy F. Woolf, writing in a October 25, 2010, analysis "Conventional Prompt Global Strike and Long Range Ballistic Missiles: Background and Issues," provides a few more possibilities for mitigating the risk of a misidentified launch. She suggests that the United States and Russia could set up a dedicated "hot line" to advise each other of non-nuclear launches; other nations could be invited to observe test launches; and increased communication between Russia and the United States could be initiated. Regardless, however, as Woolf notes, while these measures can "reduce the possibility of misunderstandings, they probably cannot eliminate them."

CPGS, while still in its early developmental stage, provides an intriguing and potentially highly valuable advancement in military weaponry. Many questions remain: How will the project be funded? How will the military judge the weapon's effectiveness? Can the technology deliver on its promises? These questions can only be answered with additional time and study.

Like CPGS, the weapons detailed in the viewpoints to follow each have their own ethical, technological, and practical considerations. For the most part, weapons are designed to kill or injure people. How military organizations and governments choose to develop and deploy such weapons is a topic thoughtful people should strive to understand more fully.

1

Nuclear Weapons Pose a Grave Threat

Malcolm Fraser

Malcolm Fraser was the prime minister of Australia from 1975 to 1983.

The large number of nuclear weapons possessed by various nations poses a serious threat to Australia and the rest of the world. Although nuclear weapons should be eliminated, nuclear power is a necessary part of the modern world; thus, the trade in nuclear fuel needs to be tightly regulated. The majority of world governments agree that nuclear weapons should be abolished and outlawed. This can be done only through a global treaty that abolishes nuclear weaponry.

Sixty-five years on from Hiroshima,[1] abolition of nukes is long overdue.

I am dismayed that the most critical security threat to Australians—the 22,600 nuclear weapons around the world—has barely rated a mention during the election campaign. Sixty-five years ago today [August 6, 2010] the city of Hiroshima and, three days later, Nagasaki were devastated by nuclear weapons. By the end of 1945, the two bombs, small by today's standards, had killed 230,000 people and injured more than 150,000.

1. The first detonation of a nuclear weapon occurred in Hiroshima, Japan, when American forces dropped an atomic bomb on August 6, 1945, effectively bringing World War II to a close.

Their radioactive poison continues to this day to afflict the survivors and their offspring with increased rates of cancer, chronic disease and genetic damage.

Nuclear Power Should Not Be Confused with Nuclear Weapons

The plea to do away with nuclear weapons should not be confused with the need to rely to a much greater extent on nuclear power for peaceful purposes. The scientific reality is that this represents an essential part of a worldwide program to combat global warming.

Australia began its trade in uranium for peaceful purposes under the most stringent safeguards, knowing that if we were in the trade, we would be able to toughen the safeguards and prevent diversion of uranium for military purposes.

The weapons currently held by nine nations are the equivalent of 150,000 times the bomb that destroyed Hiroshima.

Making the rules more rigorous, more ironclad, is an essential part of the work that lies ahead. Selling uranium to India, not a member of the nuclear non-proliferation treaty and not subject to the strictest safeguards, enabling more of its own uranium to be diverted for military purposes, runs totally counter to that objective.

The abolition of nuclear weapons and the necessary use of nuclear fuel for peaceful purposes are separate questions that should not be confused.

A Grim Reality

The grim reality of nuclear weapons is stark. In an afternoon they could lay waste much of the earth and end human civilisation. The weapons currently held by nine nations are the equivalent of 150,000 times the bomb that destroyed Hiroshima. Even a tiny fraction of the world's nuclear arsenal exploded on cities in a regional nuclear war on the other side of the world—such as between India and Pakistan, or in the Middle East—would alter the climate for years, devastating agriculture and causing starvation on a scale never seen before.

The danger of nuclear weapons being used by accident or design is growing. They and the means to acquire them—uranium enrichment technology and nuclear reactors—are spreading. If we do not get rid of them, it will only be a matter of time before the weapons are used. We must not allow that to happen.

Dismantling and outlawing nuclear weapons will need a binding, verified global treaty—as is needed to ban dumdum bullets, biological and chemical weapons, landmines and cluster bombs.

The Rudd Labor government [Australian government led by Kevin Rudd, 2007–2010] took some commendable initiatives on nuclear disarmament, establishing the International Commission on Nuclear Non-Proliferation and Disarmament and an inquiry by the all-party parliamentary joint standing committee on treaties on how Australia could best make a greater contribution to nuclear disarmament. Both made some excellent recommendations, including for negotiation of a nuclear weapons convention—a comprehensive treaty to abolish nuclear weapons. The parliamentary committee's recommendations were unanimously supported by members from the ALP [Australian Labor Party], Coalition and Greens. They provide a basis from which to move beyond counterproductive adversarial party politics to build cross-party support for humanitarian action to get rid of nuclear weapons.

Unfortunately, the government's response to both sets of recommendations has been disappointing.

Nuclear Weapons Must Be Abolished

The recently concluded five-yearly review conference on the nuclear non-proliferation treaty made it clear that the treaty by itself is inadequate to achieve the abolition of nuclear weapons. It provides no binding process and no specific phased plan. After 40 years, it has not delivered disarmament and has not prevented the proliferation of nuclear weapons. Nor has it been able to make real progress on universality, making withdrawal from the treaty more difficult, or strengthening safeguards, nuclear export controls, nuclear safety or security.

The greatest immediate threat to human survival posed by nuclear weapons affects everyone and is too important to be left to politicians.

The most significant aspect of the review conference was the unprecedented level of support from a clear majority of close to 130 of the world's governments, as well as civil society, for getting on with the negotiation of a non-discriminatory comprehensive legal framework to eliminate and outlaw nuclear weapons. Regrettably, Australia was not among them.

The greatest immediate threat to human survival posed by nuclear weapons affects everyone and is too important to be left to politicians. Citizens the world over have a critical role to play, and to ensure their leaders are in no doubt about what they must do. Leaders need to hear a multitude of voices, impossible to ignore, telling them to negotiate a global abolition treaty now. That is why I am pleased to support the MillionPleas campaign launched this week. It invites everyone to support a clear message: 65 years is too long. It's time to retire nuclear weapons. A global abolition treaty is the best way to accomplish this.

The leaders of all political parties should substantively address in their campaign policy speeches how, if elected, they will work now for negotiations to begin on a global treaty to abolish nuclear weapons.

2

Nuclear Weapons Are a Necessary Deterrent

John Hutton

John Hutton is a British Labour Party politician and a former secretary of defense for the British government.

Because of the large number of armed conflicts around the world in recent years, it is imperative for the United Kingdom to maintain a tight national security. The two main dangers to the nation include weapons of mass destruction and Islamic terrorism. Appearing weak invites such attacks. Having nuclear weapons signals strength and provides the ultimate deterrent. If other nations and terrorists have access to nuclear weapons, the United Kingdom also must have these weapons to protect its national security.

There is a growing debate in the country about how Britain can best defend itself militarily in the 21st Century.

A report last week by the Institute for Public Policy Research think-tank, questioning whether Trident nuclear submarines are a cost-effective way of maintaining the UK's nuclear deterrent, is an example of this.

But amid all the discussions, one fact stands out like a sore thumb. In the 20 years that have passed since the collapse of the Soviet Union, Britain's Armed Forces have been engaged on active service more frequently than at any time since the end of the Second World War.

There is one obvious conclusion to draw from this—that the collapse of communism did not mark the end of any threat to our national security. Far from it. And whether it is in Sierra Leone, Bosnia, Kosovo, Iraq or Afghanistan, our soldiers, sailors and airmen have demonstrated time and time again that they are the best in the world.

We should all be so proud of the work they do, day in day out. In my view, none of these conflicts was discretionary or optional. Our involvement and that of our allies was necessary to secure our vital long-term national security interests.

We should never forget that the first business of Government is national security.

National Security Is Government's First Business

We should never forget that the first business of Government is national security. Everything else is secondary. Today, the threats to our country's security are real and obvious.

Britain faces two principal dangers. Firstly from the spread of weapons of mass destruction—nuclear, chemical and biological. China, for example, is investing considerable sums in enhancing its nuclear weapons systems.

Iran is seeking a nuclear weapons capability. North Korea already has one. There are twice as many nations today that possess nuclear weapons than did so when the Nuclear Non-Proliferation Treaty was signed 41 years ago.

The second main challenge to our national security comes from Islamic terrorism—a new breed of fanaticism that despises everything we and our friends and allies stand for—liberty, human rights, equality.

Terrorists who will stop at nothing, stoop to the very depths of depravity, and use indiscriminate violence in the name of their vile cause.

We have to defend ourselves against both of these threats. We should do so because our values and freedoms are worth defending. They have been bequeathed to us by previous generations and we hold them in sacred trust for those who will come after us.

We do not have the luxury of picking and choosing which of these threats we are prepared to defend ourselves against.

If we do this, and follow the advice of some politicians, we would expose our country and our friends around the world to mortal danger. And to defend ourselves successfully, we will need, above all else, to recognise that the response to both of these threats will require different means.

Britain should always invest its principal effort in conflict prevention. It is better to prevent a war than have to fight one. It is better to prevent a state from becoming a haven for international terrorism than have to go in and flush out the terrorists.

So we should remain active in all those international security organisations that can do this vital work—the United Nations, NATO [North Atlantic Treaty Organization], the international financial institutions such as the International Monetary Fund and World Bank, and, yes, the European Union [EU] too.

We should invest more in this area. Only six percent of EU funds are devoted to conflict prevention. It is even less in the UK.

We need . . . to understand that our independent nuclear deterrent remains an absolutely essential pillar on which everything else depends.

Weakness Attracts Danger

But if all these efforts fail, then Britain must retain the ability if necessary to defend itself by all of the military means at its disposal. Weakness only attracts greater dangers. It does not make threats go away. They are there whether we like it or not, whether we choose to acknowledge it or thrust our heads in the sand.

To defend ourselves against these very different threats we need firstly to understand that our independent nuclear deterrent remains an absolutely essential pillar on which everything else depends.

It is a minimum deterrent designed to make it clear to any nuclear aggressor that we cannot and will not be blackmailed and that we will extract a terrible price if we are attacked.

Britain has done more than any other nation to show its peaceful intentions. We have reduced the number of our warheads. We have given up free-fall nuclear bombs.

Nuclear Weapons Are the Ultimate Deterrent

But we must never give up the ultimate deterrent as long as others possess nuclear weapons that could be aimed at us. So it is right that we should now be taking the necessary steps to replace our current Vanguard submarines.

The Trident missiles can be given an extended life span, providing a massively capable and cost-effective platform for decades to come.

No other delivery system—such as bombers or land-based missiles—could ever provide an equivalent level of deterrence.

Our nuclear submarines are undetectable and cannot be taken out by a pre-emptive strike. That is why they provide the best form of nuclear deterrence available to us.

It is why we should not listen to those who suggest that there is a better, cheaper form of deterrence available to us. There isn't.

It is nonsense to say that we cannot afford Trident any longer. If belts have to be tightened—and they do—this should not be done at the expense of national security. Replacing Trident will cost the equivalent of 0.1 per cent of our GDP [gross domestic product] over the lifetime of the programme. It is a price well worth paying.

Is it safe to take the risk that we can do without our own nuclear weapons while potential aggressors keep theirs?

To those who say we cannot afford the ultimate insurance policy ... I would say think again. Think about the next 50 years rather than the next 12 months and the run up to the next Election.

Who can predict what the world will look like in 50 years' time, because that is what you have to be able to do if you advocate unilateral nuclear disarmament. Politicians have many skills, but this level of foresight is well beyond our reach.

Britain Should Not Abolish Nuclear Weapons

Is it safe to take the risk that we can do without our own nuclear weapons while potential aggressors keep theirs? On the basis of what we know from the past 50 years, I say no.

Some will make the argument about the opportunity cost of proceeding with a new generation of ballistic nuclear submarines—that we have to choose between conventional capability or nuclear deterrance. This is a false argument and a false choice.

The Government has rightly made it clear that the money for replacing Trident will not come at the cost of our spending on conventional forces. So we can continue to equip our Army, the Royal Navy and the RAF [Royal Air Force] with the right equipment they need to deal with the other threats we face.

It means that in Afghanistan, for example, our troops can expect continuous improvements in their kit, and rightly so. Our Forces deserve the best that money can buy.

Predicting the future nature of armed conflict is a perilous business. No one has a good track record. That is why the best possible policy for Britain is 'safety first'.

Any politician who tells you otherwise cannot be trusted to govern.

3

Biological Weapons Pose a Serious Threat

Bob Graham, Interviewed by Matt Korade

Bob Graham was a Democratic senator from Florida who served in the US Senate from 1987 to 2005; he also was the chairman of the National Commission on the Prevention of WMD Proliferation and Terrorism. Matt Korade is a writer for Congressional Quarterly.

The National Commission on the Prevention of WMD (Weapons of Mass Destruction) Proliferation and Terrorism reported that a terrorist attack is likely, and that the weapon to be used is more likely to be biological than nuclear. Although previously terrorists have been unable to launch widespread biological attacks due to lack of knowledge, this will soon change. The United States needs to be prepared. To do this, the government must allocate sufficient funding for bio-terrorism security. America can look to the United Kingdom as a model for preparation. Pakistan is likely to be the place where terrorists will find access to biological and/or nuclear weapons.

The Senate Homeland Security and Governmental Affairs Committee approved legislation Wednesday [November 2009] that would lock down security at U.S. disease research labs and would incorporate recommendations a weapons of mass destruction commission has been making for nearly a year.

Bob Graham and Matt Korade, "WMD Commission Head: Biological Agents Remain Greatest Risk," *CQ Homeland Security*, November 4, 2009. Copyright © 2009 by CQ Roll Call Group. Reproduced by permission via Copyright Clearance Center.

In its 2008 report "World at Risk," the congressionally appointed National Commission on the Prevention of WMD [weapons of mass destruction] Proliferation and Terrorism predicted that a terrorist attack using weapons of mass destruction was "more likely than not" before 2013 and would probably involve a biological weapon. . . .

Former Sen. Bob Graham, D-Fla. (Senate, 1987–2005), the chairman of the commission, sat down recently with [reporter] Matt Korade to discuss these and other biosecurity issues.

It's more likely than not . . . that a weapon of mass destruction will be used somewhere on Earth between now [2009] and 2013.

Bioterrorism Is a Bigger Threat than Nuclear Weapons

[Matt Korade:] *I was interested in the commission's concern that bioterrorism is an even bigger threat than the nuclear issue, something to which a lot of people aren't really attuned. I was wondering what you think about both the nature of the biological threat—how big it is, why you determined it to be so, and what you're hoping people will do about it.*

[Sen. Bob Graham:] We defined the [threat] as it's more likely than not—it's better than a 50-50 chance—that a weapon of mass destruction will be used somewhere on Earth between now [2009] and 2013, and second, we thought that weapon would be a biological rather than a nuclear weapon.

Why do we think biological? For a number of reasons. There's been much more work done in securing nuclear weapons. The efforts with Russia and other former states of the Soviet Union have been ongoing now for almost 20 years and have been generally credited with being very successful. There are a limited number of nuclear weapons. You could almost put an identifying bar code on every nuclear device in the world and you'd be able to place it.

With biological weapons, there are so many more of them, there are so many more sources of production, they are significantly less difficult to develop and to use than a nuclear weapon.

The two big restraints on biological weapons have been scale and dissemination. The largest biological attack in the United States occurred in October 2001, where, according to the FBI [Federal Bureau of Investigation], a single scientist at Fort Detrick [Md.] sent a series of letters [containing Anthrax] to journalists and politicians resulting in several deaths and a number of serious illnesses and about $5 billion to $6 billion of cleanup costs. If that one scientist was working with 99 others, it would have been a much more significant event.

The second [restraint] is dissemination. There was an attack with biological weapons in Tokyo . . . a most significant, scaled attack. But they had selected an inappropriate type of the pathogen that they were using, and it was not as lethal as it could have been, and their distribution system malfunctioned.

So it's been said that our greatest safeguard has been the thin line of ignorance. That line is likely to get penetrated as terrorists become more sophisticated. We said it's more likely that a biologist will become a terrorist than a terrorist will become a biologist.

The Government Response

When you speak to the [Barack] Obama administration about this, what has been their response to your concerns? I assume they're saying it's a priority, but do you feel that's reflected in the direction the administration is taking—for example in the make-up of the reorganized National Security Council?

Yes, in the contest that this administration has started, [it has] probably the most daunting set of challenges of any administration at least since Franklin Roosevelt and in some ways even more than Franklin Roosevelt because he didn't have two foreign wars going on simultaneously with the Depression. But the president has articulated—particularly with this Prague speech and then last week at the end of the G8 [the Group of Eight nations]—his high priority and concern for this.... The fact that he's setting the stage for the 2010 Nonproliferation Treaty conference in March indicates the attention that's been given this even in spite of all these other issues.

Do you feel that the biological concern could be elevated among members of the administration and Congress?

In our report, we said that someone of gravitas should be put in charge of our WMD proliferation policy.

We have reason to believe that there is a connection between how well a country or a community is prepared and the likelihood that a terrorist will attempt the attack.

Part of that is there have been a number of issues over the last 20 years or more where there was an economic or geopolitical issue on one side of the table and, on the other side, there was increasing the likelihood of proliferation of a weapon of mass destruction. In almost every one of those instances, proliferation lost, and we felt that one of the reasons was the person who was representing the political or the economic interest tended to be a Cabinet member, like the secretary of State, the secretary of the Treasury. The person representing nonproliferation was a scientist, or a person of knowledge but not gravitas. So we felt we need to balance the table.

Jim Talent, the commission vice chairman, and myself sent a letter . . . suggesting that the office of the vice president would be the appropriate place for that responsibility, and we felt that the current occupant, [Vice President Joe Biden] was uniquely prepared in terms of his background and his demonstrated interest. . . .

Bioterrorism Is a Worldwide Threat

When you look at the range of biological threats and all the related issues of regulation and monitoring around the world, what do you see as potentially the biggest weak spot, or the biggest biological threat to U.S. nonproliferation efforts?

I'm going to answer that in the context of what the United States can do singularly. Many of the most important things are going to require high degrees of international cooperation. That's why our final report is titled "World at Risk." We want to emphasize this is not essentially a U.S. problem or a U.S. solution, it is a global problem requiring a global solution.

Having said that, what can the United States do? The single most significant thing we can do in the biological area is be prepared. We have reason to believe that there is a connection between how well a country or a community is prepared and the likelihood that a terrorist will attempt the attack. If the terrorist is aware that one country at a scale of zero to 10 is at a 9.5 in its preparation and another one is at a 2.5, the 2.5 target would be more attractive because they would be more likely to accomplish their objective.

So we're putting a lot of emphasis on that. That's why recently, when there was a proposal to divert some of the funding from what is called the Bioshield program [to other programs to prepare for the H1N1 [influenza] pandemic], we strongly objected to that because we think that's a key part to getting to the level of preparation for biological attack and will discourage the attack in the first place.

Where do you see the United States? Are we a 2.5 country? A 7.5 country?

I'd like to use a qualification. . . . I'd say that, whatever the number is, we have a significantly higher number on the nuclear side than we do on the biological side.

The Urgent vs. the Important

During the first few years of the U.S. ramp-up in biosecurity spending, there were critics working on other kinds of issues within the Department of Health and Human Services [and that] biosecurity was diverting funding that could have gone to other vital areas, including infectious disease research or cancer research, etc. How would you address those worries?

Well, I think that's a legitimate concern, and it raises the old issue of the urgent versus the important. The urgent issue tends to get dealt with first, the important takes its place in line. And certainly investment in things like cancer and other forms of large-scale, terrible diseases is an urgent problem.

We think this one is both urgent and critically important. There are few things that would be as destructive in the world as a major biological or nuclear attack. . . . In this meeting we just had, the people at the NSC [National Security Council] said they have canceled the proposal to divert money from Bioshield for H1N1. They're going to find some other source. Well, I would say the same thing for these other areas.

The answer isn't to steal from one important to fund another important program. It is to look for resources and be able to do what's in the national interest.

The feeling is that if terrorists gained access to either a biological or a nuclear device, they would use it fairly quickly.

Areas of Special Concern

When you look at the world picture on the biological WMD issue, is there a particular region of the world or a particular area that is of special concern to you?

Let me first answer the question of where I think they've done some especially positive things that we can learn from. That is the United Kingdom [UK] specifically and much of the English-speaking world generally.

The U.K. has been fighting terrorism and proliferation of weapons since World War II with a population that is approximately 20 percent of the United States'. There were more British people killed in terrorist attacks than in attacks in the United States, including 9/11, mainly by the [Irish Republican Army] over a long period of time.

They've developed some very effective mechanisms to try to deal with the immediate challenge. As an example, they've trained their garbage collectors as to what to look for in garbage cans. If they see a garbage can that has a peculiar number of boxes or bottles of chemicals they are supposed to report that.

I was told by a member of Parliament that "When these [surveillance cameras] were first put in, my constituents complained about this. Today my constituents complain if they don't have surveillance on their streets." So I think we have a lot to learn from the Brits.

Now, as to what area of the world is the most in danger, if you think that the most likely non-state perpetrator would be al Qaeda, it would be likely that the first uses would be somewhere proximate to where al Qaeda is located. The feeling is that if they gained access to either a biological or a nuclear device, they would use it fairly quickly. They would not try to warehouse it because they are not going to be able to do what North Korea is trying to do, which is build up enough of a nuclear arsenal that it can attack, accept a response and then attack again. No non-state nation is likely to be able to get into that position.

So you think perhaps in the Pakistan region?

In our report we had a whole chapter on Pakistan as being the crossroads of everything that could contribute to a terrorist getting access to a WMD.

4

Terrorists May Use Advanced Conventional Weapons

James Bonomo et al.

James Bonomo is a senior physical scientist conducting defense research and planning for the RAND Corporation. Other staff members at RAND contributed to this report.

Terrorists now have access to advanced conventional weapons utilizing new technologies. These weapons include sniper rifles with sophisticated instrumentation, long-range antitank missiles that can kill from a distance of over a mile, large limpet mines that can be attached to the hull of a ship, and precision indirect fire systems that can be directed at outdoor venues or important buildings. Using these weapons, terrorists can operate far from their targets, outside of the range that security forces can protect. As such, security forces must be on the alert and change their tactics. In addition, industry and governments must control the manufacture and usage of these weapons.

This [viewpoint] examines one manifestation of the general technical competition between terrorist groups and security organizations—the balance between the potential use by terrorists of advanced conventional weapons and the responses available to deter or counter them. Our use of the term *advanced conventional weapons* is inclusive and broad: any new or unusual conventional weaponry developed for ordinary military forces. . . . All weaponry is obviously designed to do damage, but new design features might enable new, or at least unfamiliar, terrorist attacks. At the same time, the usual limitation of weaponry to militaries implies that various controls could be applied, albeit less stringently than controls imposed upon nuclear, chemical, or biological weapons. Consequently, the competition involving advanced conventional weaponry seems both complex and potentially important.

One example of this competition has received much attention—the balance between terrorist use of man-portable air defense systems (MANPADS) and U.S. responses. The November 2002 attacks in Mombasa, Kenya, using Russian-built MANPADS against an Israeli airliner, demonstrated that terrorists are able to acquire and use that type of advanced weaponry. In response, the United States has negotiated a multinational agreement that calls for imposing both technical and procedural use controls on new MANPADS through an expansion in scope of the [2003] Wassenaar Arrangement [on Export Controls for Conventional Arms and Dual-Use Goods and Technologies]. The United States has also started a pilot program within the Department of Homeland Security to demonstrate technical countermeasures suitable for protecting commercial aircraft from MANPADS. But MANPADS are only one of a long list of advanced conventional weapons that are potentially attractive to terrorists. This [viewpoint] explores a range of other weapons, both those still under development and those already available but relatively unused by terrorists. The [viewpoint] identifies those weapons that require greater attention from U.S. homeland security decisionmakers and outlines a number of actions that can mitigate the use of these weapons by terrorists.

Key Weapons of Concern

This project identified five types of advanced conventional weapons that could, in the absence of mitigating measures, provide terrorists with a qualitatively new and different capability. Each of these weapon types threatens in some sense to change the nature of terrorist attacks:

- sniper rifles and associated instrumentation

- improved squad-level weapons of several types

- long-range antitank missiles

- large limpet mines

- precision indirect fire systems.

Sniper rifles and especially their electronic support equipment allow a relatively unskilled marksman a reasonable chance of assassinating an individual from great ranges—up to 2 km [1.2 miles]—which can be well outside the area that a security force guarding an official would consider threatening.

Improved squad-level weapons could provide a terrorist assault force with a variety of new abilities, from individual indirect fire to the ability to eliminate a strong point with a short-range, antitank weapon. Advanced armor-piercing ammunition is available for many rifles and will easily penetrate standard body armor.

Long-range, antitank weapons can destroy any vehicle and kill its occupants from beyond 2 km. These same weapons can also destroy a small building or speaking platform. Advanced versions of these weapons are further reducing demands on the operator, which may make these weapons highly attractive to terrorists.

Attacks could come from far beyond any controllable security perimeter.

Large limpet mines attached to a ship's hull have the capability to sink large, oceangoing vessels. Even smaller, more common limpet mines can sink small ships; in fact, if multiple mines are carefully emplaced, these small mines can also sink large ships. In particular, cruise ships and ferries would be vulnerable to such devices, placing their many passengers at risk. Such external mines would, of course, not be detected during conventional cargo and passenger inspections.

Finally, precision indirect fire systems—primarily advanced mortars—can enable a wide range of new terrorist attacks: on crowds in outdoor venues; on valuable physical targets, such as refineries or aircraft; and on officials or other individuals appearing at known locations, particularly in the open, such as at a press conference.

In all of these five cases, the new systems could enable the attackers to surprise security forces. The attacks could come from far beyond any controllable security perimeter, could allow a high probability of escape for the terrorists, or could require only a single, small attack to be effective.

Reducing the Threat by Raising Awareness

The first step in limiting the threat from these systems is to raise awareness of the threat. In all cases, key groups need to understand the capabilities provided by these systems. Awareness of the new capabilities should allow technical or operational changes by security forces. Such efforts may include the following key groups and threat mitigation measures:

- Personal protective services, such as the U.S. Secret Service, whose job it is to guard high-profile individuals, need to realize that snipers and antitank weapons can make lethal line-of-sight strikes from over 2 km away. They also need to realize that non-line-of-sight weapons, such as precision mortars, will soon allow very long-range, precise attacks on targets at known locations. This awareness should enable protective services to reduce opportunities for terrorists to make use of such weapons.

- Guard forces at sites and facilities need to be aware of the capabilities that new, squad-level weapons would provide to an assault force attacking them. For example, the addition of precise, indirect fire grenades should generate a greater concern with overhead cover. New rocket-propelled grenades, thermobaric warheads, and short-range antitank weapons will require enhanced fortification at strong points. Even today, currently available small-arms ammunition should motivate upgrades in guard forces' personal armor.

- Operators of cruise ships and ferries—particularly oceangoing ferries—should be aware of the potential use and impact of large limpet mines. This awareness should motivate the use of protective cordons and hull inspections before leaving port.

Reducing the Threat Through Procedural and Technical-Use Controls

Beyond awareness are procedural and technical-use controls. Most advanced conventional weapons are intended only for military use. This means that basic procedural controls governing the use of military systems will provide some limits on terrorist uses. We note two major exceptions not under such controls: sniper rifles and their accessories and advanced ammunition. For those weapons, only awareness and the precautions taken by security forces can mitigate their threat.

All the other advanced systems will presumably be subject to international procedural controls common to military systems; these controls likely will slow their diffusion to terrorist groups. But, as the preceding example of MANPADS clearly shows, even relatively expensive, controlled systems can end up in terrorists' hands.

Adding technical-use controls in many instances would represent a major step—both organizationally and technologically. First, to be effective, such technical controls require an international agreement. The continuing, complex diplomatic efforts to enhance the controls over MANPADS, where the threat has already been clearly demonstrated, illustrate the scale of any new diplomatic effort that would be required concerning other advanced weapons. We believe that to justify and to motivate such an effort would require both an increased awareness of the threatening weapon system and also readily implementable technical controls. In our view, most of the systems do not meet these two criteria.

One system, we assert, does meet both of the criteria—precision, indirect fire systems based on an advanced mortar. Many terrorists already have had some favorable experiences with mortars, notably including those terrorists being trained in the ongoing Iraqi insurgency. Because future advanced mortar systems must depend on the Global Positioning System (GPS) or an equivalent satellite system, these precision, indirect fire systems also have technical features that could facilitate various sorts of use controls. In particular, integrated electronic systems involving GPS can be designed to require a "trusted component," which would be difficult for a terrorist group to circumvent. At the same time, this trusted component would serve as the key element for technical controls. A range of limitations then becomes feasible in principle, such as the imposition of expiration times or geographic boundaries beyond which the system would not function. Importantly, these limits would be all but invisible to legitimate military users, so they would add little operational burden. But the intent of these limitations would be to make them unreliable and unattractive to most terrorist groups, particularly as unauthorized users would have no way of checking the precise times, places, or circumstances in which the system would fail.

The best time to implement such technical controls is when the system is in its design phase. Controls added "on top," after a design is "frozen," tend to be easier to circumvent.

Fortunately, the most threatening system we have identified—the GPS-guided mortar without terminal guidance—is not yet in its development phase. This situation creates an opportunity to consider ways to apply the appropriate controls. We expect that this window of opportunity will close within the next few years, however, because the military utility of and demand for such a system will be high.

Controlling Advanced Mortars Is Essential

The most worrisome advanced conventional weapons that we have identified in this research are advanced, GPS-guided mortars. Only these systems combine a significant, new capability for terrorists with a lack of effective operational counters for security forces. We must take advantage of a fleeting opportunity to design controls into the weapons. This means that starting efforts to control advanced mortars now is urgent. Although seemingly less threatening, the other advanced weapons—sniper weapons, advanced small arms, antitank guided weapons, and limpet mines—still do require some responses. Most important, they require simple awareness on the part of security forces, and also some new techniques, such as external searches of ships before leaving port.

If the United States chooses to pursue opportunities to place additional procedural and technical-use controls on precise, indirect fire weapons, such as GPS-guided mortars, we believe that two initial steps are called for. The first step is to begin diplomatic discussions with the key producer nations, so that all the involved decisionmakers and stakeholders begin evaluating potential terrorist uses of these systems. The second step is to commission a detailed study of the technical modules and architecture needed to implement proposed technical controls. Such an investigation would be directed at determining whether the existing technical modules would be sufficient or whether they might need to be modestly expanded to include the required control functions.

The U.S. Department of Homeland Security can play a key role in both these steps. Regarding the first step identified above, the department has the primary responsibility for deterring terrorist attacks. It could use that role, within the interagency process, to push for starting diplomatic discussions. This may also entail changes in the interagency system, such as permanently including the Department of Homeland Security on interagency panels that are considering arms exports. For the second step, the department could itself directly fund such a study, perhaps in concert with the U.S. National Security Agency.

While there appears to be sufficient time to negotiate and develop meaningful controls on GPS-guided mortars, that opportunity can be lost if the United States does not begin the process soon. Missing this opportunity would reduce the controls on these mortars to the existing procedural ones for military systems in general and so increase the burden on security forces to plan around and counter such attacks. Although that may be a sufficient response for the other weapon systems we have analyzed, it appears to us to be insufficient for limiting the threat from these future, advanced mortars.

5

The United States Should Sign the Ottawa Convention

Trevor Holbrook

Trevor Holbrook is an M.A.-candidate in international relations at Webster University in Bangkok, Thailand.

Landmines are used to kill or maim troops attacking a given area. After the end of a conflict, the landmines remain, presenting a serious danger to civilians who live in the area. Casualties around the world have been high. In 1997, 124 nations signed a treaty known as the Ottawa Convention calling for a worldwide ban on landmines. That number has grown to 156. The United States has not signed the document. Because America is a leader in promoting human rights and humanitarian action, and because landmines cause great harm to civilian populations, it should sign the Ottawa Convention.

The military purpose of anti-personnel landmines (APLs) is to prevent or complicate access to specific areas by killing or incapacitating enemy ground troops. Unfortunately, the vast majority of landmines used in the last several decades have been left in place following the end of conflict, posing a grave threat to local populations. Today, more than eighty million landmines remain active in over seventy countries. Since the end of the Cold War, the international community and non-governmental organizations (NGOs) have recognized the humanitarian crisis posed by landmines.

Trevor Holbrook, "U.S. Policy Recommendation: Ottawa Convention on Anti-Personnel Landmines," *Human Rights Brief*, vol. 17, no. 1, Fall 2009, pp. 24–28. Copyright © 2009 by Human Rights Brief. All rights reserved. Reproduced by permission.

Landmines Pose a Humanitarian Crisis

The scale of the landmine crisis is alarming and has both direct and secondary impacts on affected communities. Since 1975, it is estimated that over one million people have been killed or maimed by APLs, including hundreds of thousands of children. Landmine victims become a burden on their families because many can no longer work, and most require substantial medical care. In addition to the physical threat these weapons pose, their presence can have strong psychological effects and can hinder development and economic opportunities. More so than the mine itself, the threat of its presence is the underlying cause of the humanitarian crisis. Mines Advisory Group founder Rae McGrath states, "Any area suspected of being mined is a minefield until proven safe." The possibility of landmines can prevent civilians from using farmland or traveling to another village, reducing productivity and preventing trade. Moreover, mine clearance is dangerous and costly, deterring investment from mine-affected communities and preventing development. These factors keep communities trapped in poverty and insecurity, and prevent a return to normalcy for decades after a conflict ends.

A Response to the Landmine Crisis

In response to the alarming data regarding landmine casualties in the early 1990s, the International Committee of the Red Cross (ICRC) declared an epidemic and began an advocacy campaign to limit the suffering caused by these remnants of war. Growing outrage, combined with media attention, led to an unprecedented coalition of NGOs, intergovernmental organizations (IGOs), governments, and civilians calling for a global ban on anti-personnel landmines. In 1997, 124 states signed the Convention on the Prohibition of the Use, Stockpiling, Production, and Transfer of Anti-Personnel Mines and on their Destruction, otherwise known as the Ottawa Convention. The treaty combined provisions for arms control with requirements for human protection under international humanitarian law (IHL). The Ottawa Convention is aimed at eliminating the use of landmines in order to protect civilians in accordance with human rights law and IHL. Additionally, the Convention contains requirements for mine clearance and victim assistance. The goal of the International Campaign to Ban Landmines (ICBL)—a global coalition of NGOs that assisted the passage of the Ottawa Convention—and the Convention itself has been to eliminate the humanitarian landmine crisis, both through international cooperation in the humanitarian mine action effort and through the stigmatization of military landmine use.

Eleven years after opening for ratification, the [Ottawa] Convention has 156 States Parties, and international trade in landmines has virtually ceased.

As the concern over the landmine epidemic gained momentum in the early 1990s, the United States was at the forefront of the initial call for the ban. President Bill Clinton actively participated in the Ottawa Process leading up to the Convention, but ultimately refused to sign due to pressure from the Pentagon. Instead, President Clinton committed to developing alternative weapons, then banning landmine use, and signing the Ottawa Convention by 2006. However, following the administration change in 2000 and the start of wars in Afghanistan and Iraq, U.S. policy regarding landmines shifted as the international military focus turned to terrorism. In 2004, President George W. Bush announced that the United States would not sign the Ottawa Convention and would continue to produce and stockpile landmines. This stance has left the United States behind most other states, which have continued to move toward a global ban on landmines....

The Ottawa Convention Calls for a Ban on Landmines

The Ottawa Convention is considered unique in that the global humanitarian community mobilized states in the effort to ban a weapon that was actively in use throughout the world. Eleven years after opening for ratification, the Convention has 156 States Parties, and international trade in landmines has virtually ceased. Civilian casualties are almost seventy percent below levels reported in the early 1990s. While several key states such as China, Russia, India, and the United States have not signed the Convention, very few states have used landmines in the last several years as a result of increasing stigmatization. Non-signatories to the Convention are very reluctant to use mines because of the high political costs involved. In the past five years, the only governments to deploy landmines were Russia, Myanmar, and Nepal; all of whom used the mines within their own borders to fight insurgencies.

In terms of international law, the Ottawa Convention has been noted for its role in successfully incorporating the concepts of human security into the international legal framework. By using humanitarian advocacy and involving NGOs in the process, the Convention is the first treaty to eliminate a tool used for the protection of national security in favor of enhancing human security. . . .

While the Convention establishes specific timetables and guidelines for disarmament, the most important provisions are those that require states to clear all mines from their territories and ensure an ongoing commitment to assist victims and threatened populations. Furthermore, reservations are not permitted under any circumstances, preventing states from maintaining any existing minefields or stockpiles.

US Landmine Policy and Its Implications

The U.S. government has defended its decision not to sign the Ottawa Convention based on a number of factors. First, the

United States is, by a considerable margin, the world's largest financial donor to humanitarian mine action, contributing over $1.2 billion to activities in fifty countries since 1993. This funding supports mine clearance training and work, local mine risk education, victim assistance, mine-affected area surveys, and destruction of stockpiles. In many ways, these U.S. efforts surpass the requirements of the Ottawa Convention. Second, the United States has committed to using only detectable, non-persistent landmines that will self-detonate or lose power after a short period of time. Although landmines have not been used in any U.S. conflict since the 1991 Gulf War, the U.S. government still views landmines as an indispensable military tool.

Because the United States initiated the call for a landmine ban, it has been widely criticized for its refusal to accede to the Ottawa Convention.

Third, the U.S. government argues that the Ottawa Convention focuses too specifically on anti-personnel landmines while ignoring other unexploded ordnance (UXO). The United States maintains that the most effective method of controlling the UXO threat to civilians is the creation and implementation of responsible guidelines for their production, use, and subsequent removal. The Convention has been criticized for ignoring the dangers related to anti-tank mines, cluster munitions, and other UXOs. Fourth, the United States perceives the "mine-free" target of the Ottawa Convention to be an inefficient and misguided goal. The intention of the comprehensive clearance goal is to increase the international focus on mine clearance, while ensuring that areas and villages are not overlooked. The United States supports a "mine-impact free" goal which will eliminate the threat of landmines in populated areas and transportation routes, the method which it argues allows for the most cost-effective clearance of mine threats.

Finally, the U.S. government has refused to sign the Ottawa Convention because it does not allow for reservations. According to the United States, the unique situation in the demilitarized zone (DMZ) of the Korean peninsula requires the use of anti-personnel landmines in order to deter North Korean forces from entering South Korea. Without landmines, a substantially higher number of troops and weaponry would be required in Korea and more lives would be at risk. As a result, the United States has determined that the military necessity of landmines outweighs the humanitarian benefits of a total ban on anti-personnel landmines.

Accession to the [Ottawa] Convention is in the best long-term interest of the United States, allowing it to stay at the forefront of international law.

The United States Is Criticized

Because the United States has been a strong advocate for universal human rights in the past and initiated the call for a landmine ban, it has been widely criticized for its refusal to accede to the Ottawa Convention. The government clearly needs to balance its competing expectations and requirements, but the landmine issue has become politically volatile. The ICRC argues that landmines are not an indispensable military weapon and that their value is dramatically outweighed by their post-conflict effects. The stigmatization of mine use has made their political costs prohibitive. As international law moves into the arena of human security, the United States cannot afford to sacrifice its position in international affairs and international law to defend a marginally useful military tool. . . .

As a result of 12 years of competing priorities and lack of determination, the United States is preventing the full eradication of the humanitarian landmine threat. Though it seems that the trend toward human security in international law will continue to move forward without the support of the United States, the refusal of such a dominant world power stands in the way of the Ottawa Convention becoming customary international law and significantly hampers the international protection of all victims from the threat of indiscriminate remnants of war. . . .

The United States Should Sign the Ottawa Convention

While the purpose of the Ottawa Convention is clearly in line with the U.S. mission to support human rights and humanitarian action around the world, perhaps the most important reason for accession to the Convention are the treaty's implications for the future of international law. While the United States has supported the elimination of civilian landmine threats over the last twenty years, it has also continued to insist on the tactical military importance of indiscriminate anti-personnel landmines and has developed its policy based heavily on the military viewpoint. This insistence flies in the face of the international community's acknowledgement of the disproportionate humanitarian effect of such weapons and the successful introduction of the human security concept into international law. Accession to the Convention is in the best long-term interest of the United States, allowing it to stay near the forefront of international law. Possessing the technology and capability to develop new weaponry, the United States must find an alternative to landmine use in Korea. The cost of ignoring the international consensus in order to maintain a fifty-year-old war zone is short-sighted and in opposition to U.S. goals to spread freedom and improve international security.

Landmines Protect
Vulnerable Populations

Shelby Weitzel

Shelby Weitzel is a professor of philosophy at the College of the Holy Cross in Massachusetts.

Although many civilians have been killed by landmines left in place after an armed conflict, the consequences of not using landmines could be worse than using them. Opponents of land-mine use have resorted to emotional appeals rather than rea-soned argument. Evidence shows that landmines are effective weapons in warfare in that they slow down or stop the enemy. In addition, landmines protect vulnerable populations by dis-couraging attack and by protecting such populations from being overrun by armed forces. Landmines are a form of self-defense for vulnerable civilian populations, particularly in cases where they do not receive adequate protection from the police or their own governments.

People living in areas infested with landmines are quite aware of the impact these mines have on their well-being. For those of us living in "the developed world," public aware-ness of the impact of landmines is due largely to the Interna-tional Campaign to Ban Landmines [ICBL]. From this cam-paign we have learned of the physical, psychological, economic and environmental damage caused by landmines left over from past conflicts. We have also learned of ways in which,

Shelby Weitzel, "An Alternative Perspective on Landmines and Vulnerable Populations," *Journal of Mine Action*, vol. 10, no. 1, August 2006. Reproduced by permission.

contrary to the dictates of responsible use, landmines are used to terrorize civilian populations. That the most vulnerable populations in the world sustain much of this damage makes this senseless violence particularly heinous.

From what we have heard, we might easily infer that landmines are inherently problematic. However, focusing solely on these harms gives the false impression that only bad consequences result from landmine use. Furthermore, these arguments fail to consider that bad, perhaps worse, consequences can result from a *failure* to use landmines, obscuring the fact that there also have been and continue to be constructive uses for landmines with respect to vulnerable populations. I argue that landmines have *de facto* [in fact] served to protect vulnerable populations. Consequently, the wholesale stigmatization of the production and use of landmines exacerbates the vulnerability of some of the populations that the ICBL intends to protect.

Anti-Landmine Rhetoric

Genuine, open dialogue and debate regarding the production and use of landmines has been rather restricted. . . .

The strategy of ban proponents is fairly clear. According to Canadian Deputy Permanent Representative Ambassador to the United Nations Gilbert Laurin, "Meeting landmine survivors—most of them civilians and almost half of them children—is the best way to dispel forever the myth of 'responsible use' of landmines. It is the most powerful way of convincing all states that an outright ban on this weapon is the only feasible way forward."

The landmine survivors are not there merely to attract attention, although that is a necessary first step. Their plight is to be taken as a moral argument that refutes any claims that landmines can be regulated or designed to prevent such incidents in the future.

Most of us will never meet a landmine survivor; instead, we are shown graphic photos and are presented with disturbing details of their suffering. Without the photos, many people could not begin to comprehend what is at stake for a landmine victim; the images jar us from our complacency. One scholar describes this as "priming" the audience.

Those who malign the production and use of landmines seem to have overlooked what the outcome would have been without mines in many troubled regions.

Problems with the strategy emerge after the audience has been primed. The audience has not merely acquired new facts with which to make more informed judgments. Emotional reactions to the photos include shock, disgust and anger. Fortunately, these reactions urge us to help. Unfortunately, because the photos and stories are shown in the context of supporting the ICBL, the ICBL has commandeered allegiance to the victims by linking the images of the injured civilians to their agenda. The implication is that if one believes that landmines might serve useful purposes in present and future contexts, then one must not be taking seriously enough the trauma inflicted on children resulting from landmines left over from past conflicts. Believing this, many people are reticent to express skepticism. . . .

In order to properly evaluate the moral legitimacy of the use of landmines, one must do more than view vivid photos and selective statistics. Photos and sound bytes may prime an audience, but they do not constitute an argument. Those who malign the production and use of landmines seem to have overlooked what the outcome would have been without mines in many troubled regions. While the humanitarian crises resulting from decades' worth of abandoned mines are real, they should not prevent us from conducting an honest, open inquiry about the moral legitimacy of the use of landmines *per se.*

Why Landmines Are Used

The purpose of landmines and the reasons for their effectiveness in war have been clearly articulated elsewhere. Two uses are relevant here. First, landmines reduce the mobility of opponents. Second, landmines are "force multipliers," meaning they are a factor that increases the effectiveness of military force. What this means is that just about anyone can erect defensive barriers cheaply and effectively. Landmines achieve these ends because they inspire fear. The injuries sustained are particularly brutal in both the short and long term. Witnesses to the trauma are often traumatized themselves, creating a wider demoralizing effect. Hence, much of the strength of landmines lies in their obvious deterrent effect.

In the military, one does not always have the choice to avoid entering a minefield. Part of what we find so upsetting about the civilians who are injured is that they too had no real choice but to enter mined territory, whether compelled by hunger or the lack of understanding to avoid mines. But there are those people who do have a choice, namely aggressors and profiteers. In these cases people may be trying to protect their own territories from aggressors or bandits. For the mines to be effective, the would-be aggressor has to know where mines are in the area, therefore there is little to no risk of injuries sustained by landmines so long as people heed the warning. What follows are examples of contexts in which the impact of the presence of landmines is considerably more complicated than one might otherwise have thought. Although these examples are not sufficient to prove that production and use of landmines is morally justified, they do suggest that our response ought to be more nuanced than proclamations that propose nothing short of a complete ban is remotely justifiable.

Landmines Protect Vulnerable Human Populations

The ICBL has done a great service in raising awareness about the damage caused by landmines. Much of their case rests on the fact that mines do not discriminate between combatants and non-combatants. As we know, the damage extends far beyond the physical injuries themselves. The social stigma and the added economic burden that a loss of a productive person creates for victims and their families are additional harms.

Further harm results not from actual detonations, but from the belief that landmines are present in the area. The threat of mines blocks access to vital resources such as land, water, housing, public buildings, infrastructure and transport. Avoiding injury requires curtailing or refraining from securing subsistence or additional economic productivity. To make matters worse, mined roads prevent the transport of goods once collected or grown, thereby preventing income and trade.

However, while landmines can be used by someone on the outside to keep a group contained within a confined territory, so too can they be used to protect a group within a circumscribed territory by keeping dangerous persons *out*. Landmines were originally intended for purposes of defense; the fact that some now use them on the offense does not mean that landmines cease to play this defensive role.

Landmines Protect People from Armed Forces

Whether or not one believes a line between combatants and noncombatants can or should be maintained, the fact is many aggressive parties are willing to force noncombatants into their conflicts. Whether the noncombatants are "innocent" or are implicated by association and by providing indirect support to combatants, they require defense. To the extent landmines help to provide that defense, they protect children and farmers, *viz*, those people who tend to be the focal point of the humanitarian campaign to ban landmines.

If we take the moral argument against all landmine use seriously, then we have to conclude that it is wrong to use mines to defend these populations. If we join supporters of the ICBL in stigmatizing landmine use, we must also stigmatize people who want to defend these populations. We would have to stigmatize people who are glad mines are used to defend them from rape and murder. We would have to stigmatize families of soldiers who are glad that their spouses and children have one more means of ensuring that they come home.

Suppose for the moment the choice to use mines is mistaken. Even so, what this warrants is education, not vilification. But there are many cases where the choice to use mines was not mistaken; the choice to use mines saved lives. For instance, it was thick belts of landmines that protected thousands of residents in Sarajevo from meeting the same fate as Srebrenicans. Perhaps next to the photos of people who were injured by landmines, we should add the photos of women and girls who were not raped, and fathers and sons who were not removed in the night.

Landmines Provide Self Defense

Although proponents of the ICBL often work in or come from countries afflicted by landmines, the framework that they have developed does not seem to take into account all that it should. There is something wrong with the strategy to the extent that it includes vilifying those who try to protect parties who do not wish to be included in conflicts. But perhaps an even more troubling problem pertains to cases of landmine use, which the general public tends not to hear about. The way one learns of these cases is by speaking to people in the field: deminers and the people who live there. Consider the following example:

Cambodians have endured a longstanding problem with bandits. Kidnappings associated with the Khmer Rouge received attention but are now dismissed as a thing of the past. At least some of the deminers who were working in Cambodia in the 1990s know that at times it was the villagers who were laying mines to protect themselves from attack and theft by dispersed Khmer Rouge and other bandits. Travel Web sites assure us that it is now safe to travel to Cambodia. Perhaps for tourists, it is.

There are people who use mines for their own defense in the longstanding absence of adequate protection from police, the military and even the United Nations.

Let us return to the case of Sarajevo. Deminers are currently assisted by maps showing where conflicting armies deployed mines. However, their mission is considerably more difficult because not all mines were deployed by military forces. According to Dino Bulsuladzic of the University of Western Australia, "There are zones that were not mined by the military but rather by civilians themselves. One example is that of houses and gardens, more or less isolated, [that] were mined by their owners for protection out of fear of being attacked. The minefields of Sarajevo, in reality, are many more than those marked on the maps." These were civilians using mines to protect themselves while United Nations peacekeepers watched as everything these citizens held dear was being destroyed.

Landmines Help Some Communities

To demonize landmines *per se* is to demonize not only the guerrillas and the oppressive regimes that are effectively judged by their aims and methods anyway. There are people who use mines for their own defense in the longstanding absence of adequate protection from police, the military and even the United Nations. To pretend that landmines do not serve these purposes is to obfuscate the conditions of the vulnerable populations who are compelled to use them to defend themselves when no one else will.

Although people who oppose all landmine use have not caused the acute problems faced by vulnerable communities, I would suggest that the stifling of debate and the willful overlooking of such cases implicates them in terms of skewing our response to these communities. If noncombatants turn to landmines for self-protection, they must be particularly vulnerable. When the self-appointed authorities on the matter fail to acknowledge such cases exist, it makes it sound like there are no such cases, rendering the extent of their vulnerability invisible. And when we pretend landmines never help, we worsen the situation of some communities. Because by denying them recourse to an effective tool, we make them more vulnerable. And by denying ourselves recourse to an effective tool, we make it easier to give ourselves permission to claim that there is nothing we can do either.

7

Improvised Explosive Devices Are a Threat to US Armed Forces

Rick Atkinson

Rick Atkinson is a staff writer for the Washington Post.

More than 81,000 improvised explosive device (IED) attacks aimed at US military forces occurred in Iraq between 2003 and 2007, causing nearly two-thirds of the American deaths. It is difficult for US forces to combat these weapons because those who use them continually change their mode of attack. As a loosely knit guerrilla force, insurgents are more adaptable and flexible than the large military-industrial complex arming US troops. IEDs also have strategic importance in that they make soldiers nervous, damage American morale, and undermine attempts to build a stable society.

It began with a bang and "a huge white blast," in the description of one witness who outlived that Saturday morning, March 29, 2003. At a U.S. Army checkpoint straddling Highway 9, just north of Najaf, four soldiers from the 3rd Infantry Division, part of the initial invasion of Iraq, had started to search an orange-and-white taxicab at 11:30 a.m. when more than 100 pounds of C-4 plastic explosive detonated in the trunk.

The explosion tossed the sedan 15 feet down the road, killing the soldiers, the cabdriver—an apparent suicide bomber—and a passerby on a bicycle. Lt. Col. Scott E. Rutter, a battalion commander who rushed to the scene from his command post half a mile away, saw in the smoking crater and broken bodies on Highway 9 "a recognition that now we were entering into an area of warfare that's going to be completely different."

The Signature Weapon of the War in Iraq

Since that first fatal detonation of what is now known as an improvised explosive device [IED], more than 81,000 IED attacks have occurred in Iraq, including 25,000 so far this year [2007], according to U.S. military sources. The war has indeed metastasized into something "completely different," a conflict in which the roadside bomb in its many variants—including "suicide, vehicle-borne"—has become the signature weapon in Iraq and Afghanistan, as iconic as the machine gun in World War I or the laser-guided "smart bomb" in the Persian Gulf War of 1991.

IEDs have caused nearly two-thirds of the 3,100 American combat deaths in Iraq, and an even higher proportion of battle wounds.

IEDs have caused nearly two-thirds of the 3,100 American combat deaths in Iraq, and an even higher proportion of battle wounds. This year alone, through mid-July, they have also resulted in an estimated 11,000 Iraqi civilian casualties and more than 600 deaths among Iraqi security forces. To the extent that the United States is not winning militarily in Iraq, the roadside bomb, which as of Sept. 22 [2007] had killed or wounded 21,200 Americans, is both a proximate cause and a metaphor for the miscalculation and improvisation that have characterized the war.

The battle against this weapon has been a fitful struggle to regain the initiative—a relentless cycle of measure, counter-measure and counter-countermeasure—not only by discovering or neutralizing hidden bombs, the so-called fight at the roadside, but also by trying to identify and destroy the shadowy network of financiers, strategists, bombmakers and emplacers who have formed at least 160 insurgent cells in Iraq, according to a senior Defense Department official. But despite nearly $10 billion spent in the past four years by the department's main IED-fighting agency, with an additional $4.5 billion budgeted for fiscal 2008, the IED remains "the single most effective weapon against our deployed forces," as the Pentagon acknowledged this year.

The Battle Against IEDs

As early as 2003, Army officers spoke of shifting the counter-IED effort "left of boom" by disrupting insurgent cells before bombs are built and planted. Yet U.S. efforts have focused overwhelmingly on "right of boom"—by mitigating the effects of a bomb blast with heavier armor, sturdier vehicles and better trauma care—or on the boom itself, by spending, for example, more than $3 billion on 14 types of electronic jammers that sometimes also jammed the radios of friendly forces.

For years the counter-IED effort was defensive, reactive and ultimately inadequate, driven initially by a presumption that IEDs were a passing nuisance in a short war, and then by an abiding faith that science would solve the problem.

"Americans want technical solutions. They want the silver bullet," said Rear Adm. Arch Macy, commander of the Naval Surface Warfare Center in Washington, which now oversees several counter-IED technologies. "The solution to IEDs is the whole range of national power—political-military affairs, strategy, operations, intelligence."

The costly and frustrating struggle against a weapon barely on the horizon of military planners before the war in Iraq provides a unique lens for examining what some Pentagon officials now call the Long War, and for understanding how the easy victory of 2003 became the morass of 2007. . . .

As U.S. casualties spiraled from dozens to hundreds to many thousands, the quest for IED countermeasures grew both desperate and ingenious. Honeybees and hunting dogs searched for explosives. Soldiers fashioned makeshift "hillbilly armor." Jammers proliferated, with names like Warlock, Chameleon, Acorn and Duke. Strategists concocted bomb-busting techniques, such as "IED Blitz" and "backtracking" and "persistent stare."

Yet bombs continued to detonate, and soldiers kept dying. The 100 or so daily IED "events"—bombs that blow up, as well as those discovered before they detonate—have doubled since the 50 per day typical in January 2006. The 3,229 IEDs recorded in March of this year put the monthly total in Iraq above 3,000 for the first time, a threshold also exceeded in May and June. "The numbers," one Army colonel said, "are astonishing."

In Afghanistan, although IED attacks remain a small fraction of those in Iraq, the figures also have soared: from 22 in 2002 and 83 in 2003, to 1,730 in 2006 and a thousand in the first half of this year. Suicide attacks have become especially pernicious, climbing to 123 last year, according to a United Nations study, a figure that continues to grow this year, with 22 in May alone.

Insurgents have deftly leveraged consumer electronics technology to build explosive devices that are simple, cheap and deadly.

Detonating IEDs

Insurgents have deftly leveraged consumer electronics technology to build explosive devices that are simple, cheap and deadly: Almost anything that can flip a switch at a distance can detonate a bomb. In the past five years, bombmakers have developed six principal detonation triggers—pressure plates, cellphones, command wire, low-power radio-controlled, high-power radio-controlled and passive infrared—that have prompted dozens of U.S. technical antidotes, some successful and some not.

"Insurgents have shown a cycle of adaptation that is short relative to the ability of U.S. forces to develop and field IED countermeasures," a National Academy of Sciences paper concluded earlier this year. An American electrical engineer who has worked in Baghdad for more than two years was blunter: "I never really feel like I'm ahead of the game."

The IED struggle has become a test of national agility for a lumbering military-industrial complex fashioned during the Cold War to confront an even more lumbering Soviet system. "If we ever want to kneecap al-Qaeda, just get them to adopt our procurement system. It will bring them to their knees within a week," a former Pentagon official said.

"We all drank the Kool-Aid," said a retired Army officer who worked on counter-IED issues for three years. "We believed, and Congress was guilty as well, that because the United States was the technology powerhouse, the solution to this problem would come from science. That attitude was 'All we have to do is throw technology at it and the problem will go away.' . . . The day we lose a war it will be to guys with spears and loincloths, because they're not tied to technology. And we're kind of close to being there."

Or, as an officer writing in Marine Corps Gazette recently put it, "The Flintstones are adapting faster than the Jetsons."[1]

The History of IEDs

Military explosives technicians learning their craft at Eglin Air Force Base in Florida are taught that the bomb triggering the

---

1. *The Flintstones* and *The Jetsons* were popular animated television shows in the 1960s, featuring a stone-age family in the former and a space-age family in the latter.

Haymarket Riot in Chicago in 1886 was the first modern IED. T.E. Lawrence—of Arabia—wrote in "Seven Pillars of Wisdom" that roadside bombs, which mostly targeted Turkish trains in World War I, made traveling around "an uncertain terror for the enemy."

The bomb that destroyed the U.S. Marine barracks in Beirut in 1983, the truck bomb Timothy McVeigh used to kill 168 people in Oklahoma City in 1995, the devices detonated on trains in Madrid in 2004 and in the London transportation system in 2005—all were IEDs.

British troops encountered 7,000 IEDs during 30-plus years of conflict in Northern Ireland, according to a U.S. Army ordnance officer. But what the British faced in more than three decades is equivalent to less than three months in today's Iraq. Indeed, "the sheer growth of the thing," as a senior Army general put it, is what most confounds Pentagon strategists.

Insurgents often post video clips of their attacks on the Internet.

"The IED is the enemy's artillery system. It's simply a way of putting chemical and kinetic energy on top of our soldiers and Marines, or underneath them," said Montgomery C. Meigs, a retired four-star Army general who since December 2005 has served as director of the Pentagon's Joint IED Defeat Organization, the Pentagon's multibillion-dollar effort to defeat the weapon. "What's different is the trajectory. Three 152mm rounds underneath a tank, which will blow a hole in it, are artillery rounds. But they didn't come through three-dimensional space in a parabolic trajectory. They came through a social trajectory and a social network in the community."

The Strategic Importance of IEDs

Unlike conventional artillery, IEDs have profound strategic consequences, because the bomber's intent is to "bleed us in a way that attacks American political will directly and obviates the advantages we have in military forces," Meigs added. Thousands of bombs have also made U.S. troops wary and distrustful, even as a new counterinsurgency strategy expands the American military presence among the Iraqi people.

Insurgents often post video clips of their attacks on the Internet, the equivalent of taking scalps. They also exploit the Web—either openly or in password-protected sites—to share bomb-building tips, emplacement techniques, and observations about American vulnerabilities and countermeasures.

For example, a 71-page manual titled "Military Use of Electronics Prepared by Your Brother in Allah" was posted on a jihadist Web site earlier this year. Comparable in sophistication to an introductory college electrical engineering class, the manual provided color photos and detailed diagrams on "remote wirelessly operating circuit using a mobile phone for moving targets" and "employing timers to explode detonators using transistors."

The lack of success in combating IEDs has left some military officials deeply pessimistic about the future. "Hell, we're getting our ass kicked," said a senior officer at U.S. Central Command, which oversees the wars in Iraq and Afghanistan. "We're watching warfare that's centuries old being played out in a modern context and we're all confused about it. The toys and trappings have changed, but asymmetric fighting, and ambush, and deceiving and outwitting your opponent, and using the strengths of your opponent against him, are ancient."

Heartening Developments

Others point to several heartening developments. The number of IED attacks declined in Iraq late this summer after five more U.S. brigades took the field as part of a troop "surge" ordered by the White House. American casualties from IEDs also dropped. Throughout Iraq, more than half of all makeshift bombs are found before they detonate.

Moreover, improved body and vehicle armor, as well as sophisticated combat medicine, mean that the proportion of wounded U.S. soldiers to those killed in Iraq is about 8 to 1, a survivability ratio much higher than in previous wars. Also, about 70 percent of wounded soldiers return to duty within three days, according to Pentagon figures.

"We've saved a lot of lives," Deputy Defense Secretary Gordon R. England said in an interview last month. "We've had people killed and injured, but we've probably saved five or 10 times that number of people by preventing attacks, or capturing and killing [insurgents], or getting caches of weapons, or disabling them."

Fewer Casualties from IEDs

In 2003, almost every IED caused at least one coalition casualty. Now, Pentagon figures indicate, it takes four of the bombs to generate a single casualty. In addition to more aggressive attacks against IED networks, rather than simply defending against the device, various technological advances have shaped the battlefield.

The military, for example, now has about 6,000 robots, compared with a handful four years ago. And bombs detonated by radio-controlled triggers, which had become the most prominent killer of U.S. forces, today amount to only 10 percent of all IEDs in Iraq after the deployment of 30,000 jammers, with more on the way.

Still, as a "Counter IED Smart Card" distributed to American troops warns, "In Iraq, nothing is as it appears." The cycle of measure, countermeasure and counter-countermeasure continues.

Two particularly deadly IEDs now account for about 70 percent of U.S. bombing deaths in Iraq: the explosively formed penetrator, an armor-killing device first seen in May 2004, and linked by the U.S. government to Iran, and the "deep buried," or underbelly, bomb that first became prominent in August 2005.

IEDs Kill Civilians

Grievous as the IED toll has been on U.S. and coalition forces, the impact on Iraqis is greater. The Pentagon considers an explosion to be "effective" only if it causes a coalition casualty; this reflects a judgment that the strategic impact of an IED derives from its ability to erode American will, which in turn is predicated on casualties suffered by U.S. troops or their non-Iraqi allies. By this yardstick, the suicide truck bombs that killed more than 500 civilians in northwest Iraq on Aug. 14 of this year are considered "ineffective"; so, too, the IED on Sept. 13 that killed a prominent sheik in western Iraq whom President [George W.] Bush had publicly praised a week earlier for his opposition to al-Qaeda extremists.

The question occupying many defense specialists is whether the roadside bomb inevitably will appear in the United States.

Iraq's Future Depends on Reducing IEDs

But few military strategists doubt that Iraq's future depends on reducing IED attacks of all sorts. "If you can't stop vehicle-borne IEDs from being detonated in public spaces, you can't build a stable society," a Navy analyst said.

No one is ready to declare the dip in the number of bombs this summer to be an enduring decline. Insurgents appear "able to put out more IEDs to maintain that constant level of death-by-a-thousand-cuts," a senior Pentagon analyst said. "We have not seemed able to put an upper bound on that number."

And there is another mostly unspoken fear. With approximately 300 IED attacks occurring each month beyond the borders of Iraq and Afghanistan—a Pentagon document cites incidents in the Philippines, Russia, Colombia, Algeria and Somalia, among other places—the question occupying many defense specialists is whether the roadside bomb inevitably will appear in the United States in significant numbers. "It's one thing to have bombs going off in Baghdad, but it will be quite another thing when guys with vests full of explosives start blowing themselves up in Washington," said the Navy analyst. "That has all sorts of repercussions, for the economy, for civil liberties."

For now the device remains an indelible feature of the Iraqi and Afghan landscapes. "The enemy found a seam," said an Army colonel. "I don't think they knew it was a seam, but it just happened."

8

The United States Is Developing Precision Weapons of War

Sharon Weinberger

Sharon Weinberger is a national security reporter in Washington, DC.

Classified defense spending has risen to an all-time high. It appears that the spending is directed at technology that will help the military locate, track, and kill individuals and groups rather than at nuclear armament or large-scale weaponry. New projects include unmanned aircraft that can undertake spy missions manned craft cannot; tracking devices that use biological paints or mechanical sensors, or can track an individual's unique thermal pattern; and rapid-response intercontinental ballistic missiles, among others. Weapons such as these are better suited to warfare against individuals or groups than to major military operations, such as large-scale warfare.

The rise in classified defense spending [in 2011] accompanies a fundamental change in American military strategy. After the attacks of September 11, [2001,] the Pentagon began a shift away from its late Cold War-era "two-war strategy," premised on maintaining the ability to conduct two major military operations simultaneously, and began to focus instead on irregular warfare against individuals and groups. That strate-

Sharon Weinberger, "Anyone, Anywhere, Anytime: Not Since the End of the Cold War Has the Pentagon Spent So Much to Develop and Deploy Secret Weapons," *Popular Science*, vol. 277, no. 3, September 2010, pp. 44–51.

gic shift most likely coincides with an investment shift, away from technology that enables large-scale, possibly nuclear, war against superpower states and toward technology that helps military planners hunt and kill individuals. Each branch of the military uses different language to describe this process. Pentagon officials have spoken openly about their desire to use advanced technology to "reduce sensor-to-shooter time" in situations involving "time-sensitive targets." The head of U.S. Special Operations Command talks about "high-tech man-hunting," while Air Force officials describe plans to compress the "kill chain."

Even inside the Pentagon, few people know the precise details of the black budget. But by combining what is known about Pentagon goals and what is known about the most recent advances in military technology, we can begin to sketch its general contours.

Finding Targets

The first link in the kill chain: finding the person to hunt. Particularly in Afghanistan and Pakistan, this type of intelligence gathering is increasingly done using unmanned aerial vehicles (UAVs). According to the New America Foundation, a nonprofit think tank, the U.S. conducted 45 drone strikes in Pakistan in the first six months of this year. The centrality of unmanned aircraft to such missions suggests that the black budget is almost certainly already funding next-generation drones.

In April 2009, a French magazine published a photograph of one recent product of that funding—a slender-winged aircraft that had previously been spotted in southern Afghanistan and that aerospace experts had begun calling the Beast of Kandahar. After another photograph surfaced, this one a clear shot of the craft on the runway in Kandahar, the Air Force issued a statement that finally gave the Beast a formal identity: the RQ-170 Sentinel.

Manufactured by Lockheed Martin, the RQ-170 is a tail-less flying wing with the telltale shape and surface contours of a stealth aircraft. Blackplane watchers immediately noticed similarities between the RQ-170 and Lockheed's unmanned Polecat aircraft, which UAV observers had long speculated was being developed in secret and which was finally made public at the Farnborough International Airshow in England in 2006. The Air Force says that the Sentinel is a reconnaissance drone, a claim supported by the aircraft's lack of visible armaments, by the sensors that appear to be embedded in its wings, and by its "RQ" designation.

But much about the RQ-170 is puzzling. Why would the Air Force need a stealth aircraft in Afghanistan, a country with no radar defense system? It wouldn't, according to those familiar with the drone. The RQ-170 was developed with a more sophisticated enemy, perhaps China, in mind. That doesn't mean it couldn't be adapted for current conflicts, however. Unlike the relatively easy-to-spot Predator and Reaper drones, the RQ-170's stealth could allow it to conduct missions that those aircraft cannot, such as clandestine tracking, or slipping unnoticed across Afghanistan's border into Iran or Pakistan to spy on their nuclear programs.

> The [unmanned aerial drone] RQ-170's stealth could allow it to conduct missions that [larger drones] cannot, such as clandestine tracking.

Aircraft like the RQ-170, the Predator and the Reaper can get only so close to their targets, of course, which is why the Pentagon is developing micro-drones designed to investigate dangerous terrain undetected. In April the *Washington Post* reported that the CIA was using pizza-platter-size micro-drones to find insurgents in Pakistan. And the 2010 Pentagon budget contains a brief unclassified reference to Project Anubis, a micro-drone developed by the Air Force Research Laboratory.

The Air Force won't talk about that specific vehicle, but a more general 2008 marketing video released by the lab did suggest that future micro-UAVs might be equipped with "incapacitating chemicals, combustible payloads, or even explosives for precision targeting capability." The video depicts an explosives-laden drone dive-bombing and killing a sniper. Budget documents indicate that Project Anubis (named for the ancient Egyptian god of the dead) is now complete, which means a lethal micro-drone could already be in the field.

Following the Enemy

The Pentagon is forging the next link in the kill chain—following an individual—with at least one high-priority research program. The Clandestine Tagging, Tracking and Locating initiative (abbreviated both as CITL and TTL), which was conceived in 2003, is slated to get about $210 million in unclassified funding between 2008 and 2013 and may receive more than that from the black budget. "The global war on terrorism cannot be won without a Manhattan Project[1]-like TTL program," was how officials from the Defense Science Board, a civilian committee that advises the Pentagon, described the situation in a 2004 presentation, adding that "cost is not the issue."

In a 2007 briefing, Doug Richardson, an official working in the Special Reconnaissance, Surveillance, and Exploitation program in Special Operations Command, said that the Pentagon wanted to use 14 different technologies for tagging and tracking targets such as people and vehicles. Tagging could involve marking targets with invisible biological paints or micromechanical sensors; tracking would mean monitoring those markers from a distance. Other schemes entailed capturing a person's "thermal fingerprint" and then tracking him or her, perhaps from aircraft equipped with infrared sensors.

---

1. The Manhattan Project was the secret World War II program that developed the atomic bomb.

More details can be found in proposals from companies and scientists seeking Pentagon contracts. One such proposal, from a University of Florida researcher, uses insect pheromones encoded with unique identifiers that could be tracked from miles away. Other plans employ biodegradable fluorescent "taggants" that can be scattered by UAVs. Voxtel, a private firm in Oregon, has already made available a product called NightMarks, a nanocrystal that can be seen through night-vision goggles and can be hidden in anything from glass cleaner to petroleum jelly.

Other schemes entailed capturing a person's "thermal fingerprint" and then tracking him or her, perhaps from aircraft equipped with infrared sensors.

Perhaps the most advanced tagging concept is "smart dust," clouds of "motes," tiny micro-electromechanical sensors that can attach themselves to people or vehicles. Thousands of these sensors would be scattered at a time to increase the chance of at least one of them reaching its target. Kris Pister, a professor at the University of California at Berkeley, was sponsored by the Defense Advanced Research Projects Agency (Darpa), the Pentagon's R&D branch, more than a decade ago to work on smart dust and was able to create sensors the size of rice grains. In the beginning, he now says, he and his colleagues imagined "smart burrs" that could attach to a target's clothing as he or she brushed by, or "smart fleas" that could jump onto their targets. Pister says that this kind of autonomous microsensor is probably still not feasible. In 2001, however, his group succeeded in scattering more-primitive smart-dust motes from a small aerial drone and using them to track vehicles. A single UAV could easily carry thousands of tags, he says. . . .

Hitting the Target

In 1998, U.S. Navy ships in the Arabian Sea fired Tomahawk cruise missiles at a number of training camps in Afghanistan where Osama bin Laden was believed to be hiding. The missiles travel at about 550 mph, roughly the same speed as a commercial jetliner. They took more than an hour to reach their targets. If bin Laden had been in one of those camps, he had left by the time the missiles hit.

Such failures have inspired Pentagon planners to examine options that would allow them to strike precisely anywhere in the world in less than an hour, even if no drones, bombers, ships or troops were anywhere near the target. The Pentagon calls the initiative Prompt Global Strike, and in an April [2010] interview on Meet the Press, Defense Secretary Robert Gates may have admitted that the U.S. already possessed this capability. "We have, in addition to the nuclear deterrent today, a couple of things we didn't have in the Soviet days," he said. In addition to missile defense, he continued, "we have Prompt Global Strike, affording us some conventional alternatives on longrange missiles that we didn't have before." The Pentagon answered follow-up questions with silence.

By leaving the Earth's atmosphere and traveling at 15,000 mph, an intercontinental ballistic missile can reach any point in the world within 30 minutes.

Technologically, the precise, one-hour capability is not inconceivable. By leaving the Earth's atmosphere and traveling at 15,000 mph, an intercontinental ballistic missile [ICBM] can reach any point in the world within 30 minutes. Take the nuclear warhead off, and it becomes a conventionally armed Prompt Global Strike weapon. But it's not that simple. This solution places the Pentagon's current emphasis on killing individuals in direct conflict with its previous emphasis on fighting large military powers: Russian defense systems are designed to immediately detect the launch of an ICBM anywhere in the world; the government must then decide within minutes whether to retaliate. As a result, until Washington and Moscow find a way to distinguish conventionally armed ICBMs from nuclear ones, firing an ICBM at Afghanistan with the intention of killing even just one person could trigger a nuclear war.

To counter concerns that such an ICBM is heading for Russia, Pentagon officials have said that these weapons could be launched from California, where there are no nuclear-tipped missiles. (Since the placement of ICBMs is regulated by treaty and subject to inspection and verification, this system would, in theory, ensure that Moscow knows whether a missile is armed with a conventional warhead or a nuclear one. But this plan relies on Russia's trust.)

An alternative to the conventionally armed land-based ICBM is a hypersonic weapon, essentially a cruise missile capable of traveling at many times the speed of sound faster than anything in today's conventional arsenal. These missiles would not have to leave the Earth's atmosphere and would have very different trajectories from ICBMs, so Russia would be less likely to mistake them for nuclear weapons.

The Pentagon has mentioned two non ICBM candidates for Prompt Global Strike, one from the Army and one from Darpa. Both of these weapons would be boosted into the atmosphere by rockets and then glide back to Earth at hypersonic speeds. In addition to these official Prompt Global Strike options, the Pentagon is conducting at least three other hypersonic or near-hypersonic research efforts: the Air Force's X-51 WaveRider, which used a scramjet engine to accelerate to Mach 6 in May; the Navy's Revolutionary Approach to Time-Critical Long-Range Strike project, known as RATTLRS; and the Darpa-sponsored HyFly, a dual-combustion ramjet. (Ramjets and scramjets achieve rocket-like speeds without the heavy burden of liquid oxygen by mixing jet fuel with compressed air that enters the engine from the atmosphere.)

9

Music Can Be Used as a Weapon of War

David Yearsley

David Yearsley is a professor of musicology at Cornell University.

Loud music has been used as both an assault weapon and a torture device by Americans and other armies. It is effective because the ear is unable to shield itself from such attack. Interrogations occurring at Guantanamo Bay and other prisons have used loud music to encourage prisoners to talk. Because assaulting prisoners with loud music leaves no visible marks, it is a choice weapon of torturers. The Long Range Acoustic Device (LRAD) is a weapon that can project loud sound or music long distances, and was used in the Iraq War.

The human ear is defenseless. Unable to keep sound out, it must take in all it hears. Selective hearing is common phrase, but meaningless.

Musical Warfare at Waco

History's most infamous musical assault exploited the defenselessness of the ear: the massively distorted music blasted at the Branch Davidians [a religious cult] in Waco [Texas] in 1993 by the FBI [Federal Bureau of Investigation] wore down the compound dwellers over the seven week siege like a battleship pounding shoreline battlements. The final firestorm was prepared not only by sleep-preventing decibel levels but because of its horrifying aesthetic crimes, the most heinous being Nancy Sinatra's "These Boots Are Made for Walkin'." Early proponents of world music, the G-men varied their play-list with sing-along Christmas carols in saccharine 1950s style arrangements, Tibetan chants and cavalry bugle blasts. Just how seriously perpetrators of sonic violence take their music can be judged by the care with which they assemble their repertoires of destruction and despair.

Cult leader David Koresh, himself a failed pop singer, had begun the high-decibel musical exchange in Waco by first bombarding them with recordings of his own happy-clappy pop. This siege-busting tactic ceased when the federal forces cut the compound's power supply.

In Guantanamo Bay, . . . Afghanistan and Iraq, . . . interrogation techniques have involved the uses of extremely loud music by AC/DC, and Metallica as well as theme songs from children's television shows like Barney & Friends.

Waco was by no means the first instance of musical warfare. A few years before, the U.S. had tried to ferret out opera-lover Manuel Noriega from Panama City redoubt with a non-stop heavy metal bombardment: *Madame Butterfly* and *La Traviata* were no match for Black Sabbath and Judas Priest. The sonic assault was finally halted under pressure from the Vatican.

Loud Music in Torture

In Guantanamo Bay and other prisons in Afghanistan and Iraq the British rights group Reprieve has claimed that interrogation techniques have involved the uses of extremely loud music by AC/DC, and Metallica as well as theme songs from children's televison shows like *Barney & Friends*. These horrors were detailed by Andy Worthington in *Counterpunch* back in December of last year [2008].

Unfettered by earplugs, anti-noise headphones or other defensive technologies the ear is helpless to protect itself. The eyes have lids, the ears don't. In [the 1971 film] *A Clockwork Orange* when the anti-hero, the violent sociopath and Beethovenian fanatic Alex, is re-programmed to harmless passivity, his eyes must be propped open so he can be forced to witness acts of violence on the screen while being infused with a nausea-inducing drug. By contrast, the glorious sounds of Alex's beloved 9th symphony of Ludwig Van [Beethoven] accompany the images but enter unimpeded into his soul.

In the increasingly loud and intrusive modern world maybe the human earlobes will begin to evolve to become like eyelids that can be closed when things get unbearable out in the aural universe. But even this evolutionary advance wouldn't have neutralized the sub-woofers of Waco.

One of the great advantages of using music as an implement of torture is that it leaves no physical mark. As Plato and many other writers have known, music works directly on the soul. There is nothing more uplifting nor potentially devastating.

One of the great advantages of using music as an implement of torture is that it leaves no physical mark.

Music as a Battlefield Weapon

Over the past few years New York University professor of music Suzanne Cusick has been lecturing far and wide on the United States' use of music in interrogation and as a battlefield weapon. The soft-spoken, incisive Cusick came to Cornell in the spring of 2006 to deliver the year's principle music lecture, named after Donald J. Grout. Grout was one of the great music historians of the 20th century, and a deeply conservative man who would have hated every word Cusick uttered that afternoon in a corner seminar tucked in an upper floor of Cornell's music building looking out over the campus's Arts Quad and to Cayuga Lake below. Her talk concerned itself neither with the kinds of music nor the art's exalted purposes one usually discusses in the Ivory Tower.

The original title for Cusick's lecture had promised a tedious internal investigation of the discipline of musicology: "Buying (Back) the Farm, or Thoughts the Cultural Work of American Musicologies." But she changed her topic unannounced and delivered instead sixty minutes on "Music as Weapon / Music as Torture."

Much of Cusick's talk let the chilling facts speak for themselves: "On November 18, 1998, now-defunct Synetics Corporation [was contracted] to produce a tightly focused beam of infrasound—that is, vibration waves slower than 100 vps—meant to produce effects that range from 'disabling or lethal.'" In 1999, Maxwell Technologies patented a HyperSonic Sound System, another "highly directional device . . . designed to control hostile crowds or disable hostage takers." The same year Primex Physics International patented both the "Acoustic Blaster", which produced "repetitive impulse waveforms" of 165dB, directable at a distance of 50 feet, for "antipersonnel applications", and the Sequential Arc Discharge Acoustic Generator, which produces "high intensity impulsive sound waves by purely electrical means."

The Long Range Acoustic Device

She went on to describe the American Technology Corporation's development beginning some ten years ago of the Long Range Acoustic Device, or LRAD, a weapon "capable of projecting a 'strip of sound' (15 to 30 inches wide) at an average of 120 dB (maxing at 151 dB) that will be intelligible for 500 to 1,000 meters" (depending on which model you buy), the LRAD is designed to hail ships, issue battlefield or crowd-control commands, or direct an "attention-getting and highly irritating deterrent tone for behavior modification."

Wielded by the 361st PsyOps company, the LRAD was deployed to "prepare the battlefield" in the siege of Falluja [Iraq] in November of 2004. The device was armed with Metallica's "Hell's Bells" and "Shoot to Thrill."

Sonic Torture

As Cusick repeatedly pointed out, one of the great advantages of sonic weapons and torture is that they leave no mark on the victim. Guantanamo captive Binyam Mohamed, who was returned to England in February after his long years of imprisonment and torture, claimed in an interview [in] London's *Mail on Sunday* how his sonic torture began already in a Kabul prison in 2002 where he was held for eighteen months in complete darkness before his transfer to Guantanamo in 2004. His body can convey no direct physical [evidence] of this horrendous abuse, probably in contrast to the other forms of torture he suffered as in the scalpel he claims was used to sliced his genitals.

The [Long Range Acoustical Device] was deployed to "prepare the battlefield" in the siege of Falluja in ... 2004 [and] was armed with Metallica's "Hell's Bells" and "Shoot to Thrill."

In the *Mail on Sunday* interview Mohamed relates how "There were loudspeakers in the cell, pumping out a deafening volume, non-stop, 24 hours a day. They played the same CD for a month, The Eminem Show. When it was finished it went back to the beginning and started again. I couldn't sleep. I had no idea whether it was day or night."

As the *Daily Mail* is reporting today [March 13, 2009] pressure from members of parliamentary and rights groups is mounting on British Foreign secretary David Miliband to hold a judicial inquiry into Mohamed's claims that MI5 knew about the illegal torture. Indeed, U.S. crimes against international law threaten now to engulf their coalition partner on the other side of the Atlantic. In early February details of Mohamed's torture were excised from the dossier submitted to England's High Court after Miliband asserted that not doing so might be detrimental to shared U.S. and UK intelligence efforts and could "cause real and significant damage to the national security and international relations of the [UK]."

On February 22nd [2009] Prime Minister Gordon Brown insisted that there was no "cover-up" and two weeks ago Miliband and Home Secretary Jacqui Smith refused to answer questions on torture in front of the House of Commons' Joint Committee on Human Rights. Yesterday, Miliband issued a blanket denial, one which bodes ill the political future of the stonewalling foreign secretary: "We abhor torture and never order it or condone it."

Facing the Music

In the 1980s Miliband was a student at Corpus Christi College in Oxford. While there he was elected Junior Common Room President and as a result got prime rooms which happened to be located next to those of my wife, Annette Richards, similarly given housing preference because she was the college's organ scholar, discharging those duties though reading for a degree in English literature. In her rooms was a piano. Many were the nights when the studious Miliband would graciously request that she or her music-making guests stop playing because of the lateness of the hour. These were Anglican anthems or Buxtehude organ preludes not super-loud Eminem. It is now time for Miliband to face a different music.

10

Non-Lethal Weapons of War May Soon Be in Use

Randy Roughton

Randy Roughton is a senior associate editor for Airman Maga-zine, *the official magazine of the US Air Force.*

The Active Denial System (ADS) is a non-lethal weapon using electromagnetic energy beams to disperse either combatants or civilians. The beams do not injure or harm people, but they heat the skin to such an extent that those subjected to the beam be-lieve they are on fire. They quickly move to get away from the beam. The armed services believe this weapon will be highly ef-fective in bringing crowd situations under control or in delaying an attack on a trapped group of soldiers. It will also limit collat-eral damage—that is, civilians inadvertently beamed will suffer no lasting effects or harm.

An angry crowd surrounds a downed UH-60 Blackhawk [helicopter] crew in a remote province in Afghanistan. An AC-130U Spooky [an armed aircraft] flies directly above the scene, but crewmembers above can't distinguish between civil-ians and potentially deadly adversaries on the ground. Fortu-nately, in this fictional scenario, there's a new weapon on board the aircraft, one with a non-lethal beam, in addition to the platform's standard, live ammunition. Within seconds, the nonlethal weapon can disperse the crowd and clear the way for the crew's rescue.

Randy Roughton, "The Fast Goodbye," *Airman Magazine*, vol. 54, no. 5, July–August 2010, pp. 8–11. Reproduced by permission.

The "Goodbye Effect"

The Active Denial System's [ADS] non-lethal technology uses invisible beams of millimeter wave electromagnetic energy to repel potential combatants. It works from a range beyond small arms fire on the smaller ground systems and from the air on platforms such as the C-130 [military transport aircraft]. Within seconds, the beam produces what some researchers call "the goodbye effect." The phrase refers to what a person hit with the ADS feels within seconds of the heat warming his skin—an urgent desire to leave quickly and get out of the beam's path. The ground-based versions of the ADS could soon be available in deployed locations like Afghanistan and Iraq. In the past 15 years, more than 700 people have voluntarily taken hits from the directed-energy weapon in demonstrations to help prove its effectiveness and safety in a 21st century war zone. Now, it's up to the individual services to decide if they want to use the ADS and how to fund it.

An Air Force Research Laboratory [AFRL] quantum optics physicist volunteered to take an ADS strike several times. First Lt. Nathaniel T. Sorensen felt the chill of the early winter 30-degree mountain air at Kirtland Air Force Base, N.M. He waited in his short-sleeve blue uniform for the beam to hit his skin. Within two seconds the cold left Lieutenant Sorensen's mind.

This wasn't his first time as a test subject for the ADS. He also volunteered for an experiment last summer when the heat brought out an army of gnats that competed with his focus on the mission. That experiment was designed to monitor skin temperature responses to the ADS beam with an infrared camera. His job was to remain as still as possible while standing shirtless and waiting for the beam. The annoying gnats made standing still a challenge. But, the gnats quickly lost importance when the beam was trained on his skin.

"The gnats were all around me," he said. "I tried to make the best of it and pay attention. (I was) trying to count how long I could stay in the beam, or wondering if the ADS affected insects at all; anything to get my mind off the gnats in my ears. No matter how hard I tried to concentrate, as soon as the beam turned on, I couldn't pay attention to anything else at all. It opens up hot like an oven, but unlike one blast of hot air, it doesn't stop. It just keeps coming. When you have gnats flying into your ears and you don't care, you know it works."

A Non-Lethal Weapon for Peacekeeping

Officials at the research laboratory say the technology can be used for peacekeeping, area denial and riot control from above and potentially aboard a variety of aircraft in the field, while the Army may use the system on mine-resistant ambush protected vehicles. The ground-based ADS range is about 10 times greater than any other nonlethal weapon. AFRL experts expect the system will be ready for field use within two years, but the transition into the DoD [US Department of Defense] inventory can't happen until the ADS completes the acquisition process and becomes a "program of record," said Dr. Diana Loree, ADS program director.

"If a program of record is started, then demonstration systems could be fielded in less than two years," she said.

The ADS could give troops and commanders a tool allowing them time to determine the enemy's intent and reduce the enemy's immediate ability to cause harm. Loree explained that the temporary pain caused by ADS could encourage an aggressor to withdraw long enough to give that troop and commander more time to make decisions without killing or wounding anyone.

The Active Denial System Could Save Civilian Lives

Besides saving lives and buying time, it would be a huge benefit in controlling collateral damage. Loree said ADS would be very useful in repelling individuals or crowds in a specifically targeted area. That capability could add a layer of defense at entry control points, crowded villages and, if mounted on an aircraft, it could buy time for a unit if they are boxed-in or pinned down.

Staff Sgt. Adam Navin was a role player when the 820th Security Forces Group evaluated the system at Moody Air Force Base, Ga. The Airmen tested it in scenarios like securing base perimeters, inspecting suspicious vehicles, securing checkpoints and entry control points and monitoring large gatherings with the potential of violence.

He saw it as an especially effective weapon at entry control points and with large crowds. The system gave entry controllers what Sergeant Navin calls "a tight and focused beam" that allowed them to disperse a crowd of role players.

"One of the most complicated things to handle as an entry controller at a deployed location is getting the number of individuals who congest at your gate to step away or to get that same angry group to back away," Sergeant Navin said. "If this was in place, we could easily drive back those individuals while we kept the Airmen on the frontline, covered in a safe position until they had the situation handled."

The option of taking control of a potentially violent situation without firing a lethal weapon could be a major advantage.

The sergeant is a security forces apprentice course instructor with the 343rd Training Squadron at Lackland Air Force Base, Texas, and served two tours in Iraq. His observations of the ADS in action, not to mention feeling its effects firsthand, convinced him the system could be useful in Afghanistan or Iraq.

A Major Advantage

The option of taking control of a potentially violent situation without firing a lethal weapon could be a major advantage from Navin's perspective. He talked to several Airmen who employed the ADS in the training scenarios at Moody and said they felt no mixed emotions because, unlike a Taser or pepper spray, they knew the effects weren't permanent. It would just make people uncomfortable enough to move or back away.

"The value of this weapon cannot be measured," Sergeant Navin said. "In the instances where we use less than lethal force, the range and capabilities that this machine possesses far outweigh any of the current tools. Unlike a weapon that injures a person when you shoot it, this affords the users the ability to deter the threat by pure discomfort.

"Since the effects aren't lasting and it ensures limited collateral damage, the controller's mind is placed at a more sensible place of ease."

The ADS is the most heavily reviewed non-lethal weapon in DoD history. The Air Force Research Laboratory at Kirtland and the Human Effectiveness Directorate at Brooks City Base, Texas, have spent more than $50 million, on top of the millions spent by the JNLWD [Joint Non-Lethal Weapons Directorate], to ensure the ADS is effective and safe. Research has shown millimeter waves don't cause cancer or reproductive problems. Two injuries occurred in more than 11,000 ADS strikes on volunteers in the testing process. Both injuries, in 1999 and 2007, resulted in second-degree burns and were attributed to procedural errors that were corrected by hardware, software and training improvements, Loree said. The standard adverse reactions—skin blisters and reddening—are extremely rare and usually temporary.

"We've been testing for 15 years to make sure the system is just heat and doesn't cause eye or skin damage, cancer or affect reproduction," Loree said. "We want to make sure we know its effects. We're now at the point of aiding warfighters in making decisions on how to use the system, to assess the benefits of its capability versus its cost."

An energy beam from the system's millimeter waves can only penetrate 1/64 of an inch, where nerve endings are located. This is the equivalent to the thickness of three sheets of notebook paper. Microwaves can penetrate through several inches of skin. But within seconds, the ADS beam tricks the person's senses into thinking he's on fire. The system uses a transmitter to send a narrow, invisible beam of energy at the speed of light toward the subject. The beam penetrates the skin and quickly heats the surface. Within seconds, the individual feels intense heat that volunteers compare to touching a hot light bulb or a blast of hot air from an oven. However, unlike the physical effect of touching a hot bulb, there's no burning.

The system's best use is in making it impossible for an enemy to aim a weapon, or even too painful to stay in the area long enough to coordinate an attack.

A Safe Alternative to Lethal Weapons

Capt. Brian Anderson, a 37th Aerospace Dental Squadron flight surgeon, served as a medical monitor for more than 100 of the volunteer ADS subjects. He's also seen the system's reliability and effectiveness from the perspective of a medic and a volunteer.

"I've participated as a volunteer, and you get out of that beam within a second," he said. "It's completely safe, but it's painful and also a complete deterrent."

Most non-lethal weapons in the DoD inventory use kinetic energy, which has a higher injury risk and their effectiveness varies when applied to people of different ages, genders and sizes, along with drastic variations in target distance.

The ADS is consistently effective, no matter how old or big they are and there's less variation of effects with range.

"The electrically-powered beam can basically control an area causing suppression of activity, and, if necessary, discrete targeting and repelling of adversaries, even if they are in close contact with operational forces or bystanders," Loree said.

Loree explained that the system's best use is in making it impossible for an enemy, be it one or a group, to aim a weapon, or even too painful to stay in the area long enough to coordinate an attack.

Many of the 700 people who volunteered to be struck by an ADS beam are believers in its ability to make someone move.

"I am definitely of the opinion that the Active Denial System, which could make me forget about everything but the instinct to move now, even with the gnats in my ears, is an excellent device," said Lieutenant Sorensen. "There's no perfect description for something like that unless you've been shot with it. There's nothing else like it."

11

The Remote Control Killing Device Is a New Weapon of War

Jonathan Cook

Jonathan Cook is a writer and journalist based in Nazareth, Israel.

An Israeli armaments company has developed a new weapon that can be operated much like a video game from a remote location. Commonly called "Spot and Shoot," the system is operated by young Israeli female soldiers. The system's sensors transmit a real-time video picture of people near the fence along Israel's most contentious borders. The operators, with authorization from a superior officer, can shoot the intruder with remote-control machine guns. The Israeli government has been criticized for the use of this weapon on civilians.

It is called Spot and Shoot. Operators sit in front of a TV monitor from which they can control the action with a PlayStation-style joystick. The aim: to kill. Played by: young women serving in the Israeli army. Spot and Shoot, as it is called by the Israeli military, may look like a video game but the figures on the screen are real people—Palestinians in Gaza—who can be killed with the press of a button on the joystick.

The female soldiers, located far away in an operations room, are responsible for aiming and firing remote-controlled machine-guns mounted on watch-towers every few hundred metres along an electronic fence that surrounds Gaza. The system is one of the latest "remote killing" devices developed by Israel's Rafael armaments company, the former weapons research division of the Israeli army and now a separate governmental firm.

The Face of the Future

According to Giora Katz, Rafael's vice president, remote-controlled military hardware such as Spot and Shoot is the face of the future. He expects that within a decade at least a third of the machines used by the Israeli army to control land, air and sea will be unmanned. The demand for such devices, the Israeli army admits, has been partly fuelled by a combination of declining recruitment levels and a population less ready to risk death in combat.

Oren Berebbi, head of its technology branch, recently told an American newspaper: "We're trying to get to unmanned vehicles everywhere on the battlefield. We can do more and more missions without putting a soldier at risk." Rapid progress with the technology has raised alarm at the United Nations. Philip Alston, its special rapporteur on extrajudicial executions, warned last month of the danger that a "PlayStation mentality to killing" could quickly emerge.

Young women can carry out missions without breaking the social taboo of risking their lives.

According to analysts, however, Israel is unlikely to turn its back on hardware that it has been at the forefront of developing—using the occupied Palestinian territories, and especially Gaza, as testing laboratories. Remotely controlled weapons systems are in high demand from repressive regimes and the burgeoning homeland security industries around the globe. "These systems are still in the early stages of development but there is a large and growing market for them," said Shlomo Brom, a retired general and defence analyst at the Institute of National Security Studies at Tel Aviv University.

Spot and Shoot Is Operated by Women

The Spot and Shoot system—officially known as Sentry Tech—has mostly attracted attention because it is operated by 19- and 20-year-old female soldiers, making it the Israeli army's only weapons system operated exclusively by women. Female soldiers are preferred to operate remote killing devices because of a shortage of male recruits to Israel's combat units. Young women can carry out missions without breaking the social taboo of risking their lives, said Mr Brom.

The women are suppose to identify anyone suspicious approaching the fence around Gaza and, if authorised by an officer, execute them using their joysticks. The Israeli army, which plans to introduce the technology along Israel's other confrontation lines, refuses to say how many Palestinians have been killed by the remotely controlled machine-guns in Gaza. According to the Israeli media, however, it is believed to be several dozen.

It's no simple matter to take up a joystick like that of a Sony PlayStation and kill.

The system was phased-in two years ago for surveillance, but operators were only able to open fire with it more recently. The army admitted using Sentry Tech in December to kill at least two Palestinians several hundred metres inside the fence. The *Haaretz* newspaper, which was given rare access to a Sentry Tech control room, quoted one soldier, Bar Keren, 20, last week saying: "It's very alluring to be the one to do this. But not everyone wants this job. It's no simple matter to take up a joystick like that of a Sony PlayStation and kill, but ultimately it's for defence."

Audio sensors on the towers mean that the women hear the shot as it kills the target. No woman, *Haaretz* reported, had failed the task of shooting what the army calls an "incriminated" Palestinian. The Israeli military, which enforces an unmarked no-man's land inside the fence that reaches as deep as 300 metres into the tiny enclave, has been widely criticised for opening fire on civilians entering the closed zone.

New Robot Weapons

Rafael is reported to be developing a version of Sentry Tech that will fire long-range guided missiles. Another piece of hardware recently developed for the Israeli army is the Guardium, an armoured robot-car that can patrol territory at up to 80km per hour, navigate through cities, launch "ambushes" and shoot at targets. It now patrols the Israeli borders with Gaza and Lebanon. Its Israeli developers, G-Nius, have called it the world's first "robot soldier".

But Israel is most known for its role in developing "unmanned aerial vehicles"—or drones, as they have come to be known. Originally intended for spying, and first used by Israel over south Lebanon in the early 1980s, today they are increasingly being used for extrajudicial executions from thousand of feet in the sky.

12

Laser Weapons Will Defend Ships at Sea

Grace V. Jean

Grace V. Jean writes on topics of armament and weaponry for National Defense magazine.

Although lasers have been useful in targeting systems, they have not been successfully used as lethal weapons. The US Navy, however, is developing several types of laser weapons they expect to mount on ships in the near future. The lasers are capable of downing small air drones; they also will be tested on their ability to destroy high-speed boats. The laser weapons are being readied to operate successfully in rough seas. While budget constraints might limit the Navy's ability to develop more applications for the laser weaponry, research into its usefulness continues.

Military forces have been aspiring to fight at the speed of light ever since lasers were developed 60 years ago. So far, the services have succeeded in fielding lasers for targeting and other nonlethal purposes. These are helpful tools for troops on the battlefield, but far short of technologists' desire of shooting down missiles, rockets, artillery and mortar rounds with destructive light energy beams.

Harnessing high-powered lasers in a deployable weapon system has remained an elusive endeavor outside of laboratory experiments and prototyping efforts. Scientists have struggled with the paradoxical challenges of making lasers small and

Grace V. Jean, "Navy Aiming for Laser Weapons at Sea," *National Defense*, vol. 95, no. 681, August 2010, pp. 30–32. Copyright © 2010 National Defense Industrial Association. All rights reserved. Reproduced by permission.

hardy, yet powerful enough to destroy targets in seconds. Solutions are slowly forthcoming, but patience is running low for defense officials who want to start seeing results in operational settings.

The Navy Will Use Laser Weapons

The Navy expects to incorporate lasers onto most ship classes in its surface fleet, including amphibious ships, cruisers and destroyers. "The continuing goal is to deploy ships with an appropriate weapons mix, possibly one day including directed energy weapons, to engage and defeat any potential adversary across the spectrum of naval warfare," said Rear Adm. Frank Pandolfe, director of surface warfare on the Navy staff.

Experts believe that of all the services the Navy holds the most promise for helping directed energy weapons become operationally viable systems in the near future. Its warships can provide adequate spaces for hosting the current generation of power-hungry and coolant-needy lasers.

Armed with guns and missiles, the Navy's surface ships can defend themselves from current airborne and surface threats. But officials have been pushing research and development programs in directed energy in hopes of yielding future weapons to bolster ship defenses against new threats including high-speed boats and unmanned aircraft. Those efforts have blossomed into prototypes that are being tested this year [2010].

The Naval Sea Systems Command in May demonstrated the feasibility of using commercial fiber lasers to knock down small unmanned aircraft from the sky. This fall, the Office of Naval Research plans to demonstrate a high-energy laser weapon system prototype at sea for the first time. If that demonstration proves successful at destroying a high-speed boat target, then Navy officials could decide to procure a system and become the first service to incorporate high-powered lasers into its weapon inventory.

Developments in Laser Technology

Long the darlings of research laboratories and widely used in manufacturing, medicine and forensics, lasers come in a variety of wavelengths and power levels. The methods for creating and propagating those beams are often not conducive to operation in war zone environments. But recent advances in electric laser technologies are opening up some possibilities.

Lasers are generated inside a reflective optical cavity by passing light energy multiple times through a gain medium—a material in gas, liquid, solid or plasma state—which amplifies the light. Solid-state lasers rely on gain mediums comprising crystals that are "doped" with ions to help excite light particles to higher energy states.

A team from Northrop Grumman Corp. is developing a solid-state laser system for the Office of Naval Research's [ONR] maritime laser demonstration program. Powered by electricity, the system sends light through a series of microscope slide-shaped media of yttrium aluminum crystals doped with neodymium. The solid-state laser generates a 15-kilowatt beam, which is directed to the target by a set of optics designed to track the target, select an aim point and hold the beam on the aim point until the desired effect is achieved.

"It's like a high-powered sniper rifle, except with much more range," said ONR's Peter Morrison, program manager, naval air warfare and weapons department.

The laser is based upon the same technology that the Northrop Grumman team previously developed for the Defense Department's joint high-power solid-state laser program, said Dan Wildt, Northrop Grumman's vice president for directed energy systems. That program last year achieved a power level of more than 105 kilowatts—a first for solid-state lasers—and the minimum required for military weapon applications. The light ray was produced via seven laser "building blocks"—groups of 15-kilowatt laser beams that were combined into one.

For the maritime laser demonstration prototype, engineers are using an eighth chain that was built but not needed for the program's 105-kilowatt demonstration. More of the 15-kilowatt building blocks can be added to scale the maritime laser prototype power level up to address various threats, Wildt added.

Pinpoint accuracy and the ability to tailor lethality to the target give the maritime laser weapon an advantage over its kinetic energy brethren.

The maritime laser's beam control technology is derived from the Defense Department's tactical high-energy laser program, a joint U.S.-Israeli effort that yielded a prototype that shot down a total of 46 rockets, artillery shells and mortar rounds in flight. Pinpoint accuracy and the ability to tailor lethality to the target give the maritime laser weapon an advantage over its kinetic energy brethren, said Morrison.

New Lasers Can Operate in Rough Seas

Engineers beefed up the laser's optical mounts to operate in sea-state 3 environments and to survive in sea-state 5 conditions. Sea state is a scale that characterizes the frequency and height of waves. Sea-state 5 involves rough-looking waves that are eight to 13 feet tall.

The prototype in November will go to sea aboard a Navy vessel for demonstrations in the Pacific Ocean. It will shoot at small boat targets in a live-fire test area, officials said.

"This is really the first time we'll take a laser system into that realistic environment with realistic targets on a real Navy ship," said Morrison.

In a video from a previous test, the laser tracked a small boat target and maintained its crosshairs on the gunwale, or upper side edges of the vessel, at a distance of thousands of yards, Morrison pointed out.

"It's ready to operate in the maritime environment," said Wildt.

Ready for Testing

Engineers in June completed integration of the major hardware pieces. They are preparing the system for a land-based test that will fire at targets on the water prior to taking the laser to sea.

By 2016, the system could become an initial capability put onto Navy ships, said Morrison. "This is a pave-way program for Navy directed energy systems," he said. "We're definitely not talking megawatts of power, which we'll have in the future. We're not talking the most advanced [lasers] just coming out of the research labs. We're talking about advanced technology mature enough to go to that marine environment."

While developing the maritime laser, program officials looked at a large number of ship classes to evaluate whether such a system could be installed. "We found without exception that every ship class that we've looked at could accommodate an entry-level system based on this," said Wildt.

The entire laser comprises a space not much larger than a table and fits inside a standard shipping container. "We can put everything except for the beam director in an optimal spot on the ship," Wildt said. The beam director, which guides the high-energy laser onto a fine-point target, would have to be exposed to the outside environment. All of the other components can be stationed below deck.

The laser is designed to tie into the Navy's existing shipboard combat systems, where a single operator can control its operations. The operator needs specialized training, similar to the instruction that Navy crews receive for the MK 15 Phalanx close-in weapon system or the MK 45 lightweight gun. Sailors will be able to maintain the laser themselves. "It won't require a Ph.D. nuclear physicist right there babying it along," said Morrison.

A Second Type of Laser Weapon

Concurrently with the maritime laser demonstration, the Navy also is funding the development of another laser weapon system for potential shipboard use. Officials at Naval Sea Systems Command initiated a program to develop a weapon system based on commercial fiber laser technologies. Fiber lasers are solid-state lasers that rely on optic fibers as the gain medium.

Navy engineers in May used a system comprising six fiber lasers strung together to shoot down two unmanned aerial vehicles flying in the maritime environment at San Nicholas Island, Calif. The 100-kilowatt laser's electronics were integrated with the MK 15 Phalanx close-in weapon system, a 20mm rapid-fire gun found aboard most Navy ships.

The same laser last year shot down five UAVs [unmanned aerial vehicle] during a test at China Lake Naval Air Warfare Center, Calif. The UAVs were made of carbon-fiber composites that are representative of the threat, said Capt. David Kiel, program manager for directed energy and electric weapons at Naval Sea Systems Command.

The existing low-fidelity prototype could be taken to sea by the end of 2012, or the program office could build a better prototype and take that to sea by 2014, said Kiel. If funding is secured in the Navy's 2012 budget, the program office could field an initial capability as early as 2017.

The Defense Department in decades past pursued lasers to destroy supersonic targets in flight. The Navy succeeded in shooting down such targets in experiments. But the technology failed to transition to a weapon program. Other efforts, such as the Air Force's pursuit of the megawatt-class airborne laser as an anti-missile capability aboard a 747 aircraft, have been under development for years. But that program was highly criticized and eventually came under fire by Defense Secretary Robert Gates, who cut funding for a second prototype last year.

With the services under pressure to reduce spending, programs attempting to develop new weapon systems are falling under increased scrutiny. Budgetary experts warn that the Navy's maritime laser programs are no exception.

"In the present fiscal and economic climate, this is really not a propitious time for a major new weapons system like that," said Barry Watts, senior fellow at the Washington-based Center for Strategic and Budgetary Assessments. Laser weapons, he said, would be most effective against an enemy onslaught of precision weapons, such as guided missiles, rockets and mortars.

"Until something really nasty like that happens, it will be a lot of research and development and demonstrators," said Watts.

Navy officials contend that a laser weapon system could allow the service to buy fewer missiles and permit ships to access areas that may have been off-limits previously because of their traditional shipboard firepower.

In order for laser weapons to find their way onto ships, the technology has to be technically mature, affordable and fill a performance gap.

The Future of Laser Weapons

In order for laser weapons to find their way onto ships, the technology has to be technically mature, affordable and fill a performance gap, said Stan Crow, business development director for directed energy at Northrop Grumman. "Maybe it's a perfect storm right now that we haven't had before, where all three of those criteria are in place," he said.

The maritime laser team believe that the at-sea testing will demonstrate the readiness of solid-state laser weapon systems to begin transitioning to the fleet.

"The Navy is not going to procure any system that is not operationally viable," said Pandolfe. Officials are closely watching the demonstrations and will be evaluating the capability of directed energy systems against operational requirements. Lasers would not supplant existing kinetic energy systems but instead would complement them, they said. The Navy has not made any decisions so far to put lasers aboard fleet units, but a study on the future of maritime directed enemy weapon systems is ongoing.

13

Aerial Drones Serve as Weapons of War

Dan Murphy

Dan Murphy is a correspondent for The Christian Science Monitor.

Drones are remote-controlled unmanned aerial vehicles. Some drones are as small as five pounds; others are significantly larger. Small drones can be used for intelligence gathering, while larger drones can carry lethal missiles. The drones save soldiers' lives by doing dangerous work. Also, the drones have been highly successful in targeting and killing al Qaeda leaders. Although they are effective, drones sometimes present strategic problems, as their use can cause a backlash of civilian anger when civilian deaths result. One fear is that their use in Pakistan may undermine US-Pakistan cooperation in anti-terrorism efforts.

What is a drone?

Drones, or unmanned aerial vehicles (UAVs), are remote-controlled aircraft that usually carry cameras to gather intelligence and sometimes missiles to kill.

They range in size from the five-pound Raven, which is launched by an infantryman the way a child throws a paper airplane and costs $25,000 (though a full "system" consisting of three of the planes, a ground control station, and imaging equipment goes for $250,000), to the Reaper, which has a

Dan Murphy, "Briefing: Aerial Drones as Weapons of War," *Christian Science Monitor*, May 22, 2009. Copyright © 2009 by The Christian Science Monitor. All rights reserved. Reproduced by permission.

wingspan of 66 feet and is equipped with Hellfire missiles and 500-pound bombs and has a price tag of $17 million.

Though the Navy flew unmanned planes during World War II, the technology didn't catch on until the 2002 invasion of Afghanistan. Then, the US only had a handful of them. Today, there are 7,000 of them in the US arsenal.

Drones Save Soldiers

They're particularly useful in theaters like Afghanistan and the tribal areas of Pakistan, where rough terrain and hostile locals make on-the-ground intelligence gathering even tougher than normal. The key to their success is the cameras they carry— and the images they transmit instantly to infantry commanders.

Drones' great advantage is that they keep pilots and soldiers out of harm's way.

Most drones spend their days looking for improvised explosive devices along roads, flying over villages that troops may be planning to pass through, or watching houses thought to be used by militants.

Most famous are the Predators and Reapers—the missile-wielding planes that have been used to attack militants in Afghanistan and Pakistan and whose pilots are often a world away, on bases in Arizona and Nevada.

Drones' great advantage is that they keep pilots and soldiers out of harm's way. They are also much cheaper to fly than conventional planes.

"Unmanned systems are used for jobs that meet one of the three D's: dull, dirty, or dangerous," says Peter Singer, a senior fellow at the Brookings Institution in Washington [DC] and author of "Wired for War," which considers the ethical and strategic implications of the burgeoning use of UAVs and other military robots.

"The most important 'D' in my mind is 'dangerous,'" he continues. "As a commander of one of these units told me, he likes them because he doesn't have to worry about writing a letter to someone's mother."

The drones are credited with killing high-value targets in Pakistan's tribal areas.

Drones Are Effective

The lethal UAVS work as advertised. "By one count, 11 out of the top 20 [al-Qaeda] leaders we have killed by robotics, not by boots on the ground," Mr. Singer says.

The drones are credited with killing high-value targets in Pakistan's tribal areas, an effective no-go area for the US military. In January [2009], for example, a drone killed Osama al-Kini, thought to be the architect of a 2007 attack on the Marriott Hotel in Islamabad that killed 54 people.

In a sign of growing US support for drones, all branches of the military—as well as the CIA [Central Intelligence Agency]—are adopting the technology. The military spent $880 million buying such planes in 2007 and is now spending $2 billion a year on them.

In a speech at the Air War College in Alabama last month [April 2009], Defense Secretary Robert Gates said there had been a 48 percent increase in UAV patrols in combat zones in the past year, to 34 a day. Since last August [2009] the US has carried out about 40 unmanned airstrikes in Pakistan.

Drones Create Civilian Backlash

Some analysts worry that, despite the drones' tactical benefits, their heavy use could damage America's strategic goals. David Kilcullen, one of the most influential advisers in US counter-insurgency strategy in the past few years, thinks drone strikes in Pakistan do more harm than good because of the backlash they create, especially when civilians are killed.

"Unilateral strikes against targets inside Pakistan, whatever other purpose they might serve, have an unarguably and entirely negative effect on Pakistani stability," he wrote in the Small Wars Journal earlier this year.

"They increase the number and radicalism of Pakistanis who support extremism, and thus undermine the key strategic program of building a willing and capable partner in Pakistan," he continued.

The drone attacks appear to have galvanized the Taliban in Pakistan: In April their leader, Baitullah Mehsud, threatened as many as two terrorist attacks a week as long as the airstrikes continued.

Singer also points out that, while the US may hope that technological superiority will inspire fear or at least respect from enemies, to many tribal Afghans and Pakistanis the use of such weapons is seen as dishonorable because the soldiers deploying them aren't taking any risks themselves.

Drones May Undermine Pakistan's Government

The drone attacks are a clear source of public anger inside Pakistan. Leaders in Islamabad have repeatedly, even angrily, demanded that the US halt drone attacks in their country. But US officials privately say they cooperate closely in choosing targets for strikes with the Pakistani military, and that the US has tacit approval for most of its drone operations inside Pakistan's tribal areas.

Still, the airstrikes undermine the Pakistani government by setting it against the populace, which largely opposes the attacks on fellow Pakistanis.

14

Cyber Weapons Pose a Serious Threat to the United States

The Economist

The Economist *is an international weekly news magazine.*

Many government officials, politicians, and military personnel believe that the computer infrastructure of developed nations is a vulnerable target for enemies. Computers control finances, communications, industrial operations, the electrical grid, air-traffic control, and many other vital systems. An attack on these computers could completely shut down a country. Cyber-espionage, or the gathering of data about individuals and nations, is a danger to all nations. Attackers could invade the military or civilian infrastructures, threatening national security. Nations around the globe are strategizing about how to meet this growing challenge.

A re the mouse and keyboard the new weapons of conflict?

At the height of the cold war, in June 1982, an American early-warning satellite detected a large blast in Siberia. A missile being fired? A nuclear test? It was, it seems, an explosion on a Soviet gas pipeline. The cause was a malfunction in the computer-control system that Soviet spies had stolen from a firm in Canada. They did not know that the CIA had tampered with the software so that it would "go haywire, after a decent interval, to reset pump speeds and valve settings to

The Economist, "War in the Fifth Domain: Cyberwar," vol. 396, no. 8689, July 3, 2010. Copyright © The Economist Newspaper Limited, London, 2010. Reproduced by permission.

produce pressures far beyond those acceptable to pipeline joints and welds," according to the memoirs of Thomas Reed, a former air force secretary. The result, he said, "was the most monumental non-nuclear explosion and fire ever seen from space."

This was one of the earliest demonstrations of the power of a "logic bomb." Three decades later, with more and more vital computer systems linked up to the internet, could enemies use logic bombs to, say, turn off the electricity from the other side of the world? Could terrorists or hackers cause financial chaos by tampering with Wall Street's computerised trading systems? And given that computer chips and software are produced globally, could a foreign power infect high-tech military equipment with computer bugs? "It scares me to death," says one senior military source. "The destructive potential is so great."

The Fifth Domain: Cyberspace

After land, sea, air and space, warfare has entered the fifth domain: cyberspace. President Barack Obama has declared America's digital infrastructure to be a "strategic national asset" and appointed Howard Schmidt, the former head of security at Microsoft, as his cyber-security tsar. In May the Pentagon set up its new Cyber Command (Cybercom) headed by General Keith Alexander, director of the National Security Agency (NSA). His mandate is to conduct "full-spectrum" operations—to defend American military networks and attack other countries' systems. Precisely how, and by what rules, is secret.

Britain, too, has set up a cyber-security policy outfit, and an "operations centre" based in GCHQ, the British equivalent of the NSA. China talks of "winning informationised wars by the mid-21st century". Many other countries are organising for cyberwar, among them Russia, Israel and North Korea. Iran boasts of having the world's second-largest cyber-army.

What will cyberwar look like? In a new book Richard Clarke, a former White House staffer in charge of counter-terrorism and cyber-security, envisages a catastrophic breakdown within 15 minutes. Computer bugs bring down military e-mail systems; oil refineries and pipelines explode; air-traffic-control systems collapse; freight and metro trains derail; financial data are scrambled; the electrical grid goes down in the eastern United States; orbiting satellites spin out of control. Society soon breaks down as food becomes scarce and money runs out. Worst of all, the identity of the attacker may remain a mystery.

In the view of Mike McConnell, a former spy chief, the effects of full-blown cyberwar are much like nuclear attack. Cyberwar has already started, he says, "and we are losing it." Not so, retorts Mr Schmidt. There is no cyberwar. Bruce Schneier, an IT industry security guru, accuses securocrats like Mr Clarke of scaremongering. Cyberspace will certainly be part of any future war, he says, but an apocalyptic attack on America is both difficult to achieve technically ("movie-script stuff") and implausible except in the context of a real war, in which case the perpetrator is likely to be obvious.

Growing connectivity over an insecure internet multiplies the avenues for e-attack; and growing dependence on computers increases the harm they can cause.

Computers: A Blessing and a Curse

For the top brass, computer technology is both a blessing and a curse. Bombs are guided by GPS satellites; drones are piloted remotely from across the world; fighter planes and warships are now huge data-processing centres; even the ordinary foot-soldier is being wired up. Yet growing connectivity over an insecure internet multiplies the avenues for e-attack; and growing dependence on computers increases the harm they can cause.

By breaking up data and sending it over multiple routes, the internet can survive the loss of large parts of the network. Yet some of the global digital infrastructure is more fragile. More than nine-tenths of internet traffic travels through undersea fibre-optic cables, and these are dangerously bunched up in a few choke-points, for instance around New York, the Red Sea or the Luzon Strait in the Philippines. Internet traffic is directed by just 13 clusters of potentially vulnerable domain-name servers. Other dangers are coming: weakly governed swathes of Africa are being connected up to fibre-optic cables, potentially creating new havens for cyber-criminals. And the spread of mobile internet will bring new means of attack.

The internet was designed for convenience and reliability, not security. Yet in wiring together the globe, it has merged the garden and the wilderness. No passport is required in cyberspace. And although police are constrained by national borders, criminals roam freely. Enemy states are no longer on the other side of the ocean, but just behind the firewall. The ill-intentioned can mask their identity and location, impersonate others and con their way into the buildings that hold the digitised wealth of the electronic age: money, personal data and intellectual property.

The ostentatious hackers and virus-writers who once wrecked computers for fun are all but gone, replaced by criminal gangs seeking to harvest data.

Mr Obama has quoted a figure of $1 trillion lost last year to cybercrime—a bigger underworld than the drugs trade, though such figures are disputed. Banks and other companies do not like to admit how much data they lose. In 2008 alone Verizon, a telecoms company, recorded the loss of 285m personal-data records, including credit-card and bank-account details, in investigations conducted for clients.

About nine-tenths of the 140 billion e-mails sent daily are spam; of these about 16% contain moneymaking scams, including "phishing" attacks that seek to dupe recipients into giving out passwords or bank details, according to Symantec, a security-software vendor. The amount of information now available online about individuals makes it ever easier to attack a computer by crafting a personalised e-mail that is more likely to be trusted and opened. This is known as "spear-phishing".

The ostentatious hackers and virus-writers who once wrecked computers for fun are all but gone, replaced by criminal gangs seeking to harvest data. "Hacking used to be about making noise. Now it's about staying silent," says Greg Day of McAfee, a vendor of IT security products. Hackers have become wholesale providers of malware—viruses, worms and Trojans that infect computers—for others to use. Websites are now the favoured means of spreading malware, partly because the unwary are directed to them through spam or links posted on social-networking sites. And poorly designed websites often provide a window into valuable databases.

Malware is typically used to steal passwords and other data, or to open a "back door" to a computer so that it can be taken over by outsiders. Such "zombie" machines can be linked up to thousands, if not millions, of others around the world to create a "botnet". Estimates for the number of infected machines range up to 100m. Botnets are used to send spam, spread malware or launch distributed denial-of-service (DDoS) attacks, which seek to bring down a targeted computer by overloading it with countless bogus requests.

Espionage in Cyberspace

Criminals usually look for easy prey. But states can combine the criminal hacker's tricks, such as spear-phishing, with the intelligence apparatus to reconnoitre a target, the computing power to break codes and passwords, and the patience to probe a system until it finds a weakness—usually a fallible human being. Steven Chabinsky, a senior FBI official responsible for cyber-security, recently said that "given enough time, motivation and funding, a determined adversary will always—always—be able to penetrate a targeted system."

> *Spying probably presents the most immediate danger to the West: the loss of high-tech know-how that could erode its economic lead or . . . blunt its military edge.*

Traditional human spies risk arrest or execution by trying to smuggle out copies of documents. But those in the cyberworld face no such risks. "A spy might once have been able to take out a few books' worth of material," says one senior American military source, "Now they take the whole library. And if you restock the shelves, they will steal it again." . . .

"Cyber-espionage is the biggest intelligence disaster since the loss of the nuclear secrets [in the late 1940s]," says Jim Lewis of the Centre for Strategic and International Studies, a think-tank in Washington, DC. Spying probably presents the most immediate danger to the West: the loss of high-tech know-how that could erode its economic lead or, if it ever came to a shooting war, blunt its military edge.

Western spooks think China deploys the most assiduous, and most shameless, cyberspies, but Russian ones are probably more skilled and subtle. Top of the league, say the spooks, are still America's NSA and Britain's GCHQ, which may explain why Western countries have until recently been reluctant to complain too loudly about computer snooping.

Disrupting and Manipulating Data

The next step after penetrating networks to steal data is to disrupt or manipulate them. If military targeting information could be attacked, for example, ballistic missiles would be useless. Those who play war games speak of being able to "change the red and blue dots": make friendly (blue) forces appear to be the enemy (red), and vice versa.

General Alexander says the Pentagon and NSA started co-operating on cyberwarfare in late 2008 after "a serious intrusion into our classified networks". Mr Lewis says this refers to the penetration of Central Command, which oversees the wars in Iraq and Afghanistan, through an infected thumb-drive. It took a week to winkle out the intruder. Nobody knows what, if any, damage was caused. But the thought of an enemy lurking in battle-fighting systems alarms the top brass.

That said, an attacker might prefer to go after unclassified military logistics supply systems, or even the civilian infra-structure. A loss of confidence in financial data and electronic transfers could cause economic upheaval. An even bigger worry is an attack on the power grid. Power companies tend not to keep many spares of expensive generator parts, which can take months to replace. Emergency diesel generators can-not make up for the loss of the grid, and cannot operate in-definitely. Without electricity and other critical services, com-munications systems and cash-dispensers cease to work. A loss of power lasting just a few days, reckon some, starts to cause a cascade of economic damage.

Experts disagree about the vulnerability of systems that run industrial plants, known as supervisory control and data acquisition (SCADA). But more and more of these are being connected to the internet, raising the risk of remote attack. "Smart" grids, which relay information about energy use to the utilities, are promoted as ways of reducing energy waste. But they also increase security worries about both crime (eg, allowing bills to be falsified) and exposing SCADA networks to attack.

General Alexander has spoken of "hints that some pen-etrations are targeting systems for remote sabotage". But pre-cisely what is happening is unclear: are outsiders probing SCADA systems only for reconnaissance, or to open "back doors" for future use? One senior American military source said that if any country were found to be planting logic bombs on the grid, it would provoke the equivalent of the Cuban missile crisis.

Web War I

Important thinking about the tactical and legal concepts of cyber-warfare is taking place in a former Soviet barracks in Estonia, now home to NATO's "centre of excellence" for cyber-defence. It was established in response to what has become known as "Web War 1", a concerted denial-of-service attack on Estonian government, media and bank web servers that was precipitated by the decision to move a Soviet-era war memorial in central Tallinn in 2007. This was more a cyber-riot than a war, but it forced Estonia more or less to cut itself off from the internet.

Similar attacks during Russia's war with Georgia the next year looked more ominous, because they seemed to be co-ordinated with the advance of Russian military columns. Government and media websites went down and telephone lines were jammed, crippling Georgia's ability to present its case abroad. President Mikheil Saakashvili's website had to be moved to an American server better able to fight off the attack. Estonian experts were dispatched to Georgia to help out.

Many assume that both these attacks were instigated by the Kremlin. But investigations traced them only to Russian "hacktivists" and criminal botnets; many of the attacking computers were in Western countries. There are wider issues: did the cyber-attack on Estonia, a member of NATO, count as an armed attack, and should the alliance have defended it? And did Estonia's assistance to Georgia, which is not in NATO, risk drawing Estonia into the war, and NATO along with it?

Such questions permeate discussions of NATO's new "strategic concept", to be adopted later this year [2010]. A panel of experts headed by Madeleine Albright, a former American secretary of state, reported in May that cyber-attacks are among the three most likely threats to the alliance. The next significant attack, it said, "may well come down a fibre-optic cable" and may be serious enough to merit a response under the mutual-defence provisions of Article 5.

During his confirmation hearing, senators sent General Alexander several questions. Would he have "significant" offensive cyber-weapons? Might these encourage others to follow suit? How sure would he need to be about the identity of an attacker to "fire back"? Answers to these were restricted to a classified supplement. In public the general said that the president would be the judge of what constituted cyberwar; if America responded with force in cyberspace it would be in keeping with the rules of war and the "principles of military necessity, discrimination, and proportionality". . . .

One senior military official says General Alexander's priority will be to improve the defences of military networks. Another bigwig casts some doubt on cyber-offence. "It's hard to do it at a specific time," he says. "If a cyber-attack is used as a military weapon, you want a predictable time and effect. If you are using it for espionage it does not matter; you can wait." He implies that cyber-weapons would be used mainly as an adjunct to conventional operations in a narrow theatre.

Identifying attacking computers, let alone the fingers on the keyboards, is difficult.

Deterrence in Cyberwar

The Chinese may be thinking the same way. A report on China's cyber-warfare doctrine, written for the congressionally mandated US-China Economic and Security Review Commission, envisages China using cyber-weapons not to defeat America, but to disrupt and slow down its forces long enough for China to seize Taiwan without having to fight a shooting war.

Deterrence in cyber-warfare is more uncertain than, say, in nuclear strategy: there is no mutually assured destruction, the dividing line between criminality and war is blurred and identifying attacking computers, let alone the fingers on the keyboards, is difficult. Retaliation need not be confined to cyberspace; the one system that is certainly not linked to the public internet is America's nuclear firing chain. Still, the more likely use of cyber-weapons is probably not to bring about electronic apocalypse, but as tools of limited warfare.

Cyber-weapons are most effective in the hands of big states. But because they are cheap, they may be most useful to the comparatively weak. They may well suit terrorists. Fortunately, perhaps, the likes of al-Qaeda have mostly used the internet for propaganda and communication. It may be that jihadists lack the ability to, say, induce a refinery to blow itself up. Or it may be that they prefer the gory theatre of suicide-bombings to the anonymity of computer sabotage—for now.

Organizations to Contact

The editors have compiled the following list of organizations concerned with the issues debated in this book. The descriptions are derived from materials provided by the organizations. All have publications or information available for interested readers. The list was compiled on the date of publication of the present volume; names, addresses, phone and fax numbers, and e-mail and Internet addresses may change. Be aware that many organizations take several weeks or longer to respond to inquiries, so allow as much time as possible.

Arms Control Association (ACA)
1313 L St. NW, Suite 130, Washington, DC 20005
(202) 463-8270
website: www.armscontrol.org

According to its website, the Arms Control Association "is a national, nonpartisan, membership organization dedicated to promoting public understanding of and support for effective arms control policies." The group publishes the magazine *Arms Control Today* and offers analysis of arms control proposals and national security issues. The ACA website provides an extensive library of fact sheets on arms control and proliferation and chemical weapons, among other topics.

Campaign Against Arms Trade (CAAT)
11 Goodwin St., Finsbury Park, London N4 3HQ
  United Kingdom
44-020-7281-0297 • fax: 44-020-7281-4369
website: www.caat.org.uk

The Campaign Against Arms Trade is an international advocacy organization that works to end the international arms trade. It is committed to non-violence and works to change governmental policies regarding arms dealers and military purchases. The organization's website includes publications on arms fairs, companies, countries, and governments. It also includes tables and data documenting arms companies and arms exporting. *CAATnews* is a quarterly print and online magazine that includes news and analysis of weapons of war.

Center for Military Readiness
PO Box 51600, Livonia, Michigan 48151
(202) 347-5333
e-mail: info@cmrlink
website: www.crmlink.org

The Center for Military Readiness is a nonpartisan, nonprofit educational organization whose stated purpose is to promote sound military personnel policies so that the United States military is always prepared to defend the country. The organization's website has a wealth of information for students, including links to full text articles and essays.

International Campaign to Ban Landmines (ICBL)
9 Rue de Cornavin, Geneva CH1201
  Switzerland
41-022-920-0325 • fax: 41-022-9201-0115
website: www.icbl.org

The International Campaign to Ban Landmines is a Nobel Prize winning global network working to rid the world of antipersonnel landmines. The organization was largely responsible for initiating the 1997 Mine Ban Treaty. On its website, students will find the organization's newsletter; a discussion of the Mine Ban Treaty; listings of those nations that have signed the treaty and those that have not; and recommendations for making the treaty universal across the globe.

Joint Non-Lethal Weapons Program (JNLWP)
3097 Range Rd., Quantico, VA 22134-5100
(703) 784-1977
e-mail: webmaster@jnlwp.usmc.mil
website: www.jnlwp.usmc.mil

The Joint Non-Lethal Weapons Program is a subdivision of the US Department of Defense (DoD). The organization is responsible for the identification, evaluation, recommendation, and development of non-lethal weapons. As such, the JNLWP website is the DoD's central resource for information on non-lethal weapons. On the website, students will find descriptions of a variety of non-lethal weapons, including the Active Denial System; photos; discussion of the effects of non-lethal weapons on humans; and links to other resources.

Nuclear Threat Initiative
1747 Pennsylvania Ave. NW, 7th Floor
Washington, DC   20006
(202) 296-4810 • fax: (202) 296-4811
e-mail: contact@nti.org
website: www.nti.org

According to its website, the mission of the Nuclear Threat Initiative "is to strengthen global security by reducing the risk of use and preventing the spread of nuclear, biological and chemical weapons." Chaired by former US senator Sam Nunn and philanthropist Ted Turner, the organization includes members from around the world. The website includes a plethora of publications, papers, information, and news releases, including "Deterrence: Its Past and Future," remarks by Senator Nunn delivered at a 2010 conference. The group also sponsors the Global Security Newswire, providing daily headline news.

Organisation for the Prohibition of Chemical Weapons
Johan de Wittlaan 32, The Hague   2517 JR
   The Netherlands
3170-416-3300 • fax: 3170-306-3535
website: www.opcw.org

The Organisation for the Prohibition of Chemical Weapons is the body responsible for implementing the Chemical Weapons Convention, a treaty that bans the use of chemical weapons.

The group's website includes the text of the Chemical Weapons Convention as well as listings of those nations who are signatories and those who are not. In addition, the website also includes news articles, fact sheets regarding chemical weapons, a history of the organization, and a glossary.

Union of Concerned Scientists
National Headquarters, 2 Brattle Square
Cambridge, MA 02138-3780
(617) 547-5552 • fax: (617) 864-9405
website: www.ucsusa.org

The Union of Concerned Scientists is a nonprofit organization composed of scientists who work for environmental issues and world safety. Members conduct and analyze scientific research as well as advocate for policy changes that will provide solutions for some of the world's most pressing problems. Its website includes a great deal of information concerning nuclear weapons and nuclear war. In addition to news articles and links, its publications include *Securing the Skies: 10 Steps the United States Should Take to Improve the Security and Sustainability of Space* (2010), the most recent of their reports. Other publications include *Catalyst* magazine and *Earthwise* newsletter, both available on the website.

US Army
1400 Defense Pentagon, Washington, DC 20301-1400
website: www.army.mil

The US Army is the branch of the military responsible for defense and warfare on land. The Army employs many weapons of war. On the Army's website, students can access *Soldiers* magazine, *The NCO Journal*, and many Army newspapers published around the country. In addition, the Army maintains a professional writing collection with articles from a variety of military journals.

US Department of Defense (DoD)

1400 Defense Pentagon, Washington, DC   20301-1400
(703) 571-3343
website: www.defense.gov

The US Department of Defense is the division of the government in charge of all military personnel in all branches as well as the National Guard and Reserve. The DoD website provides news releases, press advisories, photos, videos, and speeches concerning national defense and weaponry, and various military information.

US Navy

Chief of Information, Department of Navy
1200 Navy Pentagon, Room 4B463
Washington, DC   20350-1200
website: www.navy.mil

The US Navy is the branch of the military responsible for defense and warfare on sea and to a lesser extent, in the air. The Navy's website includes issues of *All Hands*, a historic publication, as well as contemporary magazines and newsletters. Fact sheets on the website include listings of all aircraft, guns, missiles, ships, and other weapons of war under the command of the Navy.

US Strategic Command

Public Affairs Office (J020), 901 SAC Blvd., Suite 1A1
Offutt Air Force Base, Nebraska   68113-6020
(402) 294-4130
e-mail: pa@stracom.mil
website: www.stratcom.mil

According to its website, the US Strategic Command is the agency charged with providing global security for America by deterring attacks; ensuring US freedom of action in space and cyberspace; and planning and executing strategic deterrence operations, among other responsibilities. On the organization's website, students will find descriptions of various missions; a history of the Strategic Command; descriptions of weapons; news releases; and a wide variety of fact sheets regarding US security. In addition, a helpful FAQ page will answer many questions about the Strategic Command and its mission.

Bibliography

Books

William H.
Boothby

Weapons and the Law of Armed Conflict. New York: Oxford University Press, 2009.

Richard A. Clarke
and Robert K.
Knake

Cyber War: The Next Threat to National Security and What to Do About It. New York: Ecco, 2010.

Anne L. Clunan
and Peter R.
Lavoy

Terrorism, War or Disease? Unraveling the Use of Biological Weapons. Stanford, CA: Stanford Security Studies, 2008.

Matt Doeden

Weapons of the Modern Day. Mankato, MN: Capstone Press, 2008.

H. Bruce Franklin

War Stars: The Superweapon and the American Imagination. Amherst, MA: University of Massachusetts Press, 2008.

Gregory D.
Koblentz

Living Weapons: Biological Warfare and International Security. Ithaca, NY: Cornell University Press, 2009.

Jeffrey Alan
Lockwood

Six-Legged Soldiers: Using Insects as Weapons of War. New York: Oxford University Press, 2009.

Richard Rhodes

Arsenals of Folly: The Making of the Nuclear Arms Race. New York: Knopf, 2007.

Richard Rhodes *The Twilight of the Bombs: Recent Challenges, New Dangers, and the Prospects for a World Without Nuclear Weapons.* New York: Alfred A. Knopf, 2010.

Andrew Jon Rotter *Hiroshima: The World's Bomb.* New York: Oxford University Press, 2008.

Jonathan Schell *The Seventh Decade: The New Shape of Nuclear Danger.* New York: Metropolitan Books, 2007.

P.W. Singer *Wired for War: The Robotics Revolution and Conflict in the Twenty-First Century.* New York: Penguin, 2009.

Periodical and Internet Sources

Richard Clarke "The War from Cyberspace," *The National Interest*, vol. 104, November–December 2009, pp. 31–36.

Tom Daschle and Tom Inglesby "Foreword: Necessary Progress in Biosecurity," *Harvard Law and Policy Review*, vol. 4, no. 2, Summer 2010, pp. 263–270.

The Economist "The Militarisation of Space: Disharmony in the Spheres," vol. 386, no. 8563, January 17, 2008, p. 26.

Sandra I. Erwin "Air Force: To Save Fuel, We Must Change How We Fly," *National Defense*, vol. 95, no. 680, July 2010, pp. 16–17.

Jean V. Grace — "Research Challenge: How to Defend Against Still-Undefined Chemical, Biological Attacks," *National Defense*, vol. 94, no. 679, June 2010, pp. 38–39.

Paul K. Kerr — "Nuclear Biological, and Chemical Weapons and Missiles: Status and Trends," *CRS Report for Congress*, Congressional Research Service, February 20, 2008. www.fas.org/sgp/crs/nuke/RL30699.pdf.

Patrick Leahy — "The Way Forward on Anti-Personnel Landmines," May 18, 2010. leahy.senate.gov/press/press_releases/release/?id=fa683 dd6-7e22-4fa4-b4e6-565abb715cd4.

Miguel Marin-Bosch — "A Nuclear-Weapons Free-World: Is It Achievable?," *UN Chronicle*, vol. 46, no. 1–2, March–June 2009, pp. 36–40.

Brian Mockenhaupt — "We've Seen the Future, and It's Unmanned," *Esquire*, vol. 152, no. 5, November 2009, pp. 130–138.

Sam Nunn — "Taking Steps Toward a World Free of Nuclear Weapons," *Daedalus*, Fall 2009, pp. 153–156.

Michael O'Hanlon — "Is a World Without Nuclear Weapons Really Possible?" *The Chronicle of Higher Education*, vol. 56, no. 34, May 2, 2010.

Stamatios A. Papadakis et al.   "Anti-Personnel Landmine Injuries During Peace: Experience in a European Country," July–August 2006, pp. 237–240.

Joe Papparlardo   "The Future for UAVs in the US Air Force," *Popular Mechanics*, February 26, 2010. www.popularmechanics.com/technology/aviation/military/4347306.

Gerard Powers   "The Nuclear Ethics Gap: Finding Our Way on the Road to Disarmament," *America*, vol. 202, no. 16, May 17, 2010, pp. 10–14.

Laura Sanders   "Safety in Numbers," *Science News*, vol. 178, no. 2, July 17, 2010, pp. 18–21.

Chris Schneidmiller   "US Eliminates 80 Percent of Chemical Weapons Arsenal," *Global Security Newswire*, October 5, 2010. www.globalsecuritynewswire.org/gsn/nw_20101005_5357.php.

The Scotsman   "Leader: New Weapons Needed to Combat New Dangers," October 19, 2010.

Craig Whitlock   "US Looks to Non-Nuclear Weapons to Use as Deterrent," *The Washington Post*, April 8, 2010.

Robert Wilkie   "Hybrid Warfare: Something Old, Not Something New," *Air and Space Power Journal*, Winter 2009, pp. 13–17.

Col. Yao Yunzhu   "China's Perspective on Nuclear Deterrence," *Air and Space Power Journal*, Spring 2010, pp. 27–30.

Index